REVELATION
Interpreting the Prophecy

Let the word of Christ dwell in you richly as you teach and admonish one another with all wisdom, and as you sing psalms, hymns and spiritual songs with gratitude in your hearts to God (Colossians 3:16).

Prepared by Dale E. Griffin and Julene Dumit
Edited by Rodney L. Rathmann

SAINT LOUIS

Contents

Introduction

Advance Preparation

To get the most out of group Bible study, you should first study the lesson alone. (But if you are not able to do your advance preparation, come to the group study anyway. You will still benefit.)

Begin your private study time with prayer. God's Word is no ordinary book. Written by inspiration of the Holy Spirit (See **2 Timothy 3:16**), this is God's message to *you*.

Read the chapters of **Revelation** designated for the lesson in the New International Version of the Bible and in any other versions you have available.

Allow time for God's message to sink in. Meditate upon the Word. Underline in your Bible the passages that are especially meaningful to you at the moment. Make notes in the margin. Put a question mark beside passages that you need to study further.

Remember that the Bible interprets itself. When one passage of Scripture is not clear to you, let another passage of Scripture explain it to you. Jesus gave an example of how to do this in **Matthew 19:3–9.** He refers to **Genesis 2:24** in order to explain **Deuteronomy 24:1.**

Search for the Holy Spirit's meaning. Ask yourself these three questions: What does it say? What does it mean? What does it mean to me? Let the message go from your head to your heart to your life.

Write down your answers to the lesson's questions in this Study Guide.

Studying God's Word Together

A Bible study group needs a time and place to meet. An informal setting in a home or church where the group can sit in a circle or around a table is most desirable.

Some groups meet for an hour once a week; other groups meet every other week. Find the time and frequency that best suits your particular group. The important thing is that you make an opportunity to study God's Word together.

You may select one member of the group as leader or each member of the group may take a turn as leader. The purpose of the leader is to encourage each member of the group to participate in the discussion, to give direction to the discussion, and to keep the group moving forward to its goal at each session.

Each Bible study session should begin with an opening devotion. Especially pray for the power and presence of the Holy Spirit. The leader should make arrangements for the opening devotions for each lesson but need not do it personally each time.

The leader will direct the group to the aim of each lesson. It's like aiming your arrow at the target's bull's-eye. Then discuss the need or want presented. Draw out group discussion by such questions as, "Have you ever had a similar experience?" "How do you feel about this situation?" etc. Be on the lookout for the shy member who needs to be encouraged to share.

As you study God's Word together, you may wish to read some passages from other translations or paraphrases, but note that the questions are based on the wording in the New International Version of the Bible. Since the sections of Scripture are long, it is very important to study them prior to the class. Share your answers to the questions. When you share a truth, it helps others to grow in their faith. You may often find it challenges your own life even more.

Be sure to allow sufficient time to discuss at least several of the questions that apply God's Word to the lives of the participants. As the truths of God's Word are applied to human lives, changes will occur. "For the word of God is living and active. Sharper than any double-edged sword, it penetrates even to dividing soul and spirit, joints and marrow; it judges the thoughts and attitudes of the heart" **(Hebrews 4:12).** The Holy Spirit works through the Word to cause our faith in Jesus Christ, our Savior, to grow. This faith shows itself in the life of every believer through the fruit of the Spirit **(Galatians 5:22–23).**

Note: A group may decide, because of the length of some lessons, to divide the material into two or more sessions.

Approaches to the Interpretation of Revelation

Several general approaches to the interpretation of **Revelation** have been used fairly frequently. The *preterist* approach focuses on **Revelation's** first-century setting and sees the fulfillment of its major prophecies in the fall of Rome. The *historicist* approach sees **Revelation** as a forecast of events in human history from the first century until the end of the world. The *futurist* view is that **Revelation** primarily describes events that will happen near the end of this age. The *idealist* approach regards **Revelation** as an expression of timeless truths that govern the history of the world and the church.

All of these approaches have something to say to us as we seek to interpret **Revelation.** This book was originally addressed to a first-century situation, but it also deals with events from the time of Christ until the end. We are encouraged to look forward to the Last Day when the victorious Lamb will appear visibly to all humanity to usher in the new eternal age.

Certainly, we can discover in this book certain principles that describe how God rules and guides all human history.

As we approach **Revelation,** it is crucial to note that we do not have a document that proceeds in a linear, chronological way from beginning to end. Rather, John uses a cyclical approach. In each of a number of cycles, John reveals (1) something of what will occur throughout the New Testament era from the time of Jesus until the end of the world and (2) something of what will occur at the very end. Each cycle is from a different angle, emphasizing different things. And each culminates with the end of this age.

Cycles and recurring themes are also characteristic of Old Testament literature (e.g., the creation described in two complementary chapters in **Genesis 1–2**; the poetry of the psalms; Daniel's two visions of the four coming kingdoms in **Daniel 2** and **7**). This approach is also used by John in his gospel and first epistle (see the outline of these books in the Concordia Self-Study Bible).

John makes extensive use of the Old Testament in **Revelation.** While rarely quoting directly, John creates a mosaic using word patterns, phrases, and thoughts from the Old Testament Scriptures. Your study of this book will be enriched if you make use of the cross reference section of your Bible, as well as looking up the Old Testament references in this study.

Reference Materials

Your study of **Revelation** will be enhanced if your group has access to at least one and preferably several good commentaries to consult as you work through this study. The following are recommended:

Becker, Siegbert W. *Revelation*. Milwaukee: Northwestern, 1985. (An excellent, popular, dependable commentary.)

Caird, G. B. *A Commentary on the Revelation of St. John the Divine*. New York: Harper and Row, 1966. (A standard commentary conservative in interpretation but somewhat liberal in theology.)

Franzmann, Martin H. *The Revelation to John*. St. Louis: Concordia, 1976. (A brief, popular, verse-by-verse commentary.)

Hendriksen, W. *More Than Conquerors: An Interpretation of the Book of Revelation*. Third Printing. Grand Rapids: Baker, 1944. (An excellent, popular, theological exposition of Revelation.)

Lenski, R. C. H. *The Interpretation of St. John's Revelation.* Columbus: Lutheran Book Concern, 1935. (Although one may not agree with all of the author's conclusions, this is a conservative, useful book.)

Morris, Leon. *The Book of Revelation: An Introduction and Commentary.* Revised Edition. Tyndale New Testament Commentaries. Grand Rapids: Eerdmans, 1969, 1987. (A conservative, balanced, readable commentary.)

Poellot, Luther. *Revelation: The Last Book in the Bible.* St. Louis: Concordia, 1962. (A popular study of Revelation originally offered to a Bible class in a congregational setting.)

Swete, Henry B. *The Apocalypse of St. John.* Third Edition. London: MacMillan, 1908. Reprinted by William B. Eerdmans, Grand Rapids, 1968. (One of the best technical commentaries.)

In addition, you may wish to consult books on New Testament introduction and Bible dictionaries for background material on the book.

Lesson 1

Introducing Revelation and Its Author

Who Wrote Revelation?

1. According to **Revelation** itself, who is the author **(1:1, 4, 9; 22:8)**?

2. Look up the following references and write a few brief notes to supply background information about the identity of the person generally accepted as the author of this book.

a. **Mark 1:19–20—**

b. **Luke 9:28–29—**

c. **John 13:23—**

d. **John 18:15—**

e. **John 19:26–27—**

f. **John 20:1–10—**

g. **John 21:1–7—**

h. **Acts 3:1–10—**

3. Were John the sole author of this book, we would rightly hesitate to believe or accept it. It might seem to be merely an account of dreams or nightmares experienced by the writer. According to the following pas-

sages, by what authority did John write: **Revelation 1:1–3, 10–11; 2:7; 14:13; 22:16?**

For Whom Was Revelation Written?

In referring to "the seven churches in the province of Asia" **(1:4),** John seems to be indicating that this was to be a circular letter to be read throughout the Roman province of Asia. The seven churches were those in major cities, and they likely served as centers for the distribution of copies of this letter.

During the first centuries, the Christian church was centered around the eastern end of the Mediterranean Sea. When **Revelation** was written, Asia Minor was a major center of Christianity. Its six provinces (Asia, Bithynia [including Pontus], Galatia, Cappadocia, Cilicia, Lycia [including Pamphylia]) seem to have been among the wealthiest parts of the Roman Empire at the time. This area of Asia was conquered by the king of Pergamum with the help of the Romans early in the second century before Christ.

The Roman province of Asia was created in 129 B.C. out of the lands bequeathed to the Roman Senate by Attalus III, the last king of Pergamum. It was approximately 300 by 260 miles—an area comparable in size to that of Nebraska or South Dakota. The seven cities addressed in **Revelation** were centers of wealth, power, and culture.

By the Christian era, Judaism had been well established in Ephesus **(Acts 18:19)** and presumably in most of the other cities in this province. Probably Christianity was first brought to this area by those who on Pentecost had been converted to Jesus Christ **(Acts 2:5–11).** Paul, the missionary apostle, evidently did not spend much time in the province of Asia until his third missionary journey (ca. A.D. 53–57).

Quite early in their existence these churches needed the encouragement such as that offered by John in **Revelation.** Already in the early 50s Paul encountered the fanatical devotion of the Ephesian populace to Artemis and the commercial advantage that accrued from this pagan cult **(Acts 19:23–41).** Soon thereafter the Roman emperor Nero (A.D. 54–68) made Christians the scapegoat for his own growing unpopularity in the empire. Peter and Paul were victims of the Neronian persecution of the church. A few scholars believe that it was in the face of this persecution that John wrote his letter of encouragement to the Christians in Asia.

However, the majority of scholars believe that this letter was precipitated by the second widespread persecution of Christians in the empire—that initiated by Domitian. It was under Domitian that the cult of emperor worship became widespread throughout the empire. Domitian regarded himself as being "Lord and God" and demanded the worship of people throughout his domains. Those who refused were regarded as enemies of the state and were subjected to torture and death. John himself was exiled from Ephesus to Patmos. It was to people in this situation that John penned this epistle.

The book itself clearly identifies the immediate recipients of this letter in **Revelation 1:4.** These seven churches are identified specifically in **Revelation.** Look up these verses and write the names of the cities on the map. Refer to the maps in the back of a good study Bible if you need help.

1. **2:1**
2. **2:8**
3. **2:12**
4. **2:18**
5. **3:1**
6. **3:7**
7. **3:14**

The Seven Churches

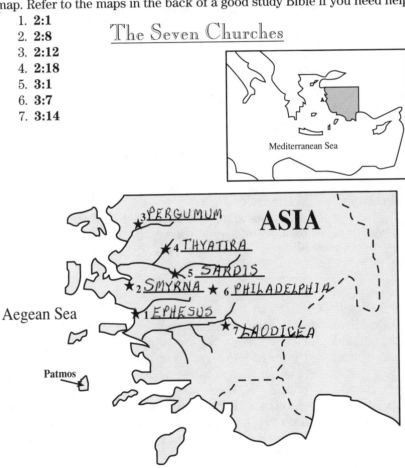

Mediterranean Sea

ASIA

3 PERGUMUM

4 THYATIRA

5 SARDIS

2 SMYRNA   6 PHILADELPHIA

Aegean Sea

1 EPHESUS

7 LAODICEA

Patmos

The Purpose of the Letter

A primary purpose of the letter was to encourage Christians in every age who must suffer because of their faith in and allegiance to Jesus Christ as their only Lord and Savior.

The overarching theme of **Revelation** is to unveil for Christians of every age, including those of first-century Asia, the reign of Jesus Christ *now* amid all the enmity of the world. It offers to suffering believers a philosophy of history. Although it may seem that Satan and evil rule this universe, God is still in control. Our Savior who lived among us for our redemption has ascended to the Father. There He, with the Father and the Holy Spirit, rules all things both now and forever. Therefore, we can live each moment, in spite of all difficulties, in joy and confidence because our Lord God reigns!

But that is not all. **Revelation** points us to a brighter future. In this book the Lord Jesus reveals to us in a small measure the glory, blessedness, and joy that we can anticipate in a new, eternal age to come. We can greet each day, no matter how dark it may seem, with the assurance of Jesus and the prayer of John, " 'Yes, I am coming soon.' Amen. Come, Lord Jesus" (**Revelation 22:20**).

Revelation is also a missionary book. It reveals to us our purpose as Christians in this world. We have been called by God to be His instruments. By the working of His Spirit through the Word, He overcomes the forces of evil in this world and draws people from every nation into the glorious company of His saints.

The placing of **Revelation** at the end of our Bible is most appropriate. This book is the capstone of all Scripture; it points us to our ultimate, final destiny in which we share with Jesus His eternal exaltation with the Father.

Type of Literature

In the opening words, John identifies this book as an *apocalypse* (revelation, unfolding, unveiling). The word *apocalyptic* is generally used for a writing whose stated purpose is to reveal or unveil the secrets of the future that God has in store for humanity. Apocalyptic literature developed after the exile and has roots in Old Testament prophetic literature, especially **Isaiah 24–27; Zechariah 9–14;** and portions of **Ezekiel; Joel;** and **Daniel.** Following are some aspects of apocalyptic literature in general.

1. *It is eschatological.* It tells of a future period of time when God will break into this world of time and space to bring everything to a final reckoning.

2. *It is dualistic.* It depicts good versus evil, God versus Satan. There are no gray areas—only black and white.

3. *It is pessimistic.* It gives up all hope for peace and righteousness on earth.

4. *It is characterized by a divine plan.* In this plan everything is moving forward according to a predetermined schedule.

5. *It uses pictures, symbols, and allegories, giving special significance to numbers and colors.*

6. *It is pseudonymous.* In the nonbiblical apocalyptic literature, the author often claims to be a great figure from Old Testament history who received the message in a vision or otherworldly journey. Usually an angel interprets the vision for the author or serves as a guide on the journey.

These characteristics especially fit the apocalyptic books that were written between 200 B.C. and A.D. 100. Many of these books are not part of Scripture. They include the Book of Enoch, the Book of Jubilees, the Assumption of Moses, and 4 Esdras. **Revelation** is different from these apocalyptic books in several important ways.

1. **Revelation** is not pseudonymous; the author of the book is clearly identified (**Revelation 1:1, 4, 9; 22:8**).

2. **Revelation** is a book of prophecy (**Revelation 1:3; 22:7, 10, 18–19**).

3. John was not pessimistic. Although evil and Satan run rampant in this present age, God is still in control. The exalted Christ is present among His people and rules all things for the ultimate welfare of His followers. The Lamb has obtained for His people victory over Satan, sin, death, and hell (**Revelation 12:10–12**). In the eternal age to come, God's people will join Christ in His exalted state of perfect joy and bliss.

4. Similarly, John had a different view of history than do apocalyptic writers in general. For many such writers the present age is evil and without meaning—a transitory interlude prior to the all-important end of all things. For John this present age that lies between Christ's sojourn on earth and His second coming is a time of God's redemptive activity in history.

Through the proclamation of the Gospel by His people, God is waging a war against the forces of Satan that will culminate with complete victory at the end of this age. In spite of the evil we experience as we fulfill this task, we can be assured of the presence and power of the victorious Lamb to sustain us and give us the final victory.

5. John did not claim to write merely on the basis of a vision. He was fully conscious, lifted by the Spirit into a different mode of existence. He not only saw the visions; he experienced them.

6. Although angels play an important role in many apocalyptic writings, the place of angels in **Revelation** is distinctive. Jesus Christ is the angel (the messenger) of this revelation, although He also uses created angels to accomplish His purposes.

The Symbolic Language of Revelation

The use of symbols was widespread in the Old Testament world (e.g., **Ezekiel**), as well as in the Hellenistic world. Although the symbolic language of **Revelation** causes us some difficulties, the symbols were probably much more readily known to the original readers and hearers. In his commentary on **Revelation,** Siegbert Becker gives the following helpful information about interpreting symbolic language:

> Symbolic and figurative language must never be pressed beyond the point of comparison. That does not mean that the symbols are arbitrary and can be interpreted any way at all. There is a reason why the Savior is described as a lamb and the devil is pictured as a great red dragon. Those who remember that the Savior told his disciples to let their light shine will know why the seven golden candlesticks are used as symbols for the seven churches. *We will have learned how to deal with this book when we have learned to read the Apocalypse the way we read the parables* (pp. 15–16).

In the ancient world, grotesque symbols always symbolized something supernatural. Symbols common to everyday life were used to say something about human nature. At times the grotesque was combined with symbols from everyday life to indicate the entry of the supernatural into the everyday lives of people (e.g., **Revelation 13:17**).

When using symbols, a writer usually took entities generally known among his readers so that they could relate to them. Out of this the writer created new meanings. For example, Jews of the first century still regarded the Babylonian captivity with horror, a horror akin to that which the Holocaust holds for present-day Jews. So John used Babylon to represent the satanic power and evil of Rome and also for all future satanic powers that would persecute the people of God.

For Discussion

1. What might the people of God in the world today consider to be their "Babylon"?

2. Give examples of forms of persecution faced by you and the other Christians in your community.

3. Of what promises of God can we remind ourselves in the face of persecution **(Romans 8:35–39)?**

The Use of Numbers

Numbers are prominently used in **Revelation** and can be the source of much irresponsible interpretation and heated discussion. But John's original readers knew what these numbers meant. Here are a few of these meanings to help you understand **Revelation** better.

Three refers to God; He is three persons in one essence.

Four represents the natural creation.

Six refers to humankind, created on the sixth day of creation.

Seven symbolizes completeness. It also represents God working's through the Holy Spirit among His people.

Ten stands for total earthly power; it also symbolizes totality or completeness.

Twelve is used either for the people of God in the Old Testament or in the New Testament (the 12 tribes of ancient Israel; the 12 apostles).

Twenty-four represents the whole church of both the Old Testament and the New Testament (the 12 tribes plus the 12 apostles).

One thousand represents the highest completeness (10 x 10 x 10 = 1,000).

For Next Time

Read **Revelation 1:1–3:22.**

To Him who loves us and has freed us from our sins by His blood, and has made us to be a kingdom and priests to serve His God and Father—to Him be glory for ever and ever! Amen. Revelation 1:5–6

Lesson 2

Preparing for the Truth

Bible Basis
Revelation 1:1–3:22

Introduction

At the very beginning of the Apocalypse, God through John prepared his audience for what would be disclosed. First, John established his credentials and authority for what he was about to describe (**Revelation 1:1–20**). Second, he prepared his hearers to receive his message with the proper disposition and attitude (**Revelation 2:1–3:22**). Then, as we shall see in the next lesson, he described the inaugural vision that provides the setting and background for the visions yet to come (**Revelation 4:1–5:14**).

Prolog and Doxology

1. As you read the prolog to this letter (**Revelation 1:1–3**), answer these questions.

a. Who is the ultimate source of this letter (**1:1**)?

b. For what purpose was this revelation given (**1:1, 3**)?

c. What further information about the theme and purpose of this book is given in **2:10; 22:20**?

d. Through whom was this vision revealed to the writer **(1:1–2)**? According to **1:2,** what was it that was revealed to the writer?

e. What probably was the coming crisis ("the time is near," **v. 3**) for which the writer wanted to prepare the hearers?

2. Read **Revelation 1:4–8.** Remembering that seven is the symbol for completeness, what might it indicate that God chose seven churches to receive this letter?

3. The three persons of the Trinity are mentioned in **verses 4–5.** The seven spirits before God's throne is a reference to the Holy Spirit in the fullness of His power and activity. **Isaiah 11:2** alludes to the sevenfold gifts of the Spirit.

Recall that three is the number that symbolizes God, and note the three-fold structure of what is said about God the Father and about Jesus.

Explain the description of God the Father provided in **verse 4** (see also **Exodus 3:14**).

4. How is Jesus described?

5. What has Jesus done for us and made us **(vv. 5b–6)**?

6. The world does not now perceive the supreme reign of Christ over all things. When will that become evident to all (see **Daniel 7:13–14; Matthew 24:30–31; Acts 1:9–11**)?

7. Why will people mourn when Jesus returns? Note the expression of certainty at the end of **verse 7.**

8. Commentators do not agree whether the speaker in **verse 8** is God the Father or Jesus. In either case, what does it mean that the speaker is the Alpha and the Omega?

9. What comfort do **verses 4–8** provide for God's people experiencing persecution?

John's Call to His Prophetic Mission

Read **Revelation 1:9–20.** In beginning this account of his commissioning, John makes the interesting observation that he shares with his fellow believers "the suffering and kingdom and patient endurance that are ours in Jesus" **(v. 9).** Even as the divine Jesus reigned also while on the cross, so His people live and reign in and with Him even in the midst of suffering and death.

1. One Lord's Day while in exile on Patmos, John was carried by the Spirit into eternity, where he saw what is and what will be from the view of God Himself. The first thing John heard was a loud voice. What did this voice tell John to do **(vv. 11, 19)**?

2. When John turned to see who was speaking, he saw one "like a son of man" standing among seven golden lampstands. What was John's reaction to what he saw **(v. 17)?** What moved John to do this?

3. What reassurance did the figure give John **(vv. 17–18)?**

4. Although this figure is not named, how do you know it was Jesus?

5. What do the seven stars and the seven golden lampstands represent **(v. 20)?**

The Letters

Each church faced specific temptations that might lead them away from God—especially in the day of persecution and martyrdom. In these letters Jesus prepared the Christians for impending persecution and assured them of divine power, protection, and blessing. It must be noted that Christians in every generation face similar situations and temptations and they too have the Lord's presence, promise, and protection to see them through.

Each letter is structured around several common elements:

1. Identification of the group being addressed
2. A description of specific qualities of Christ usually drawn from material in the first chapter
3. Praise (except for Laodicea) for the church's good record
4. Identification of the dangers peculiar to that church
5. A call to repentance
6. A Gospel promise in the setting of the Last Day

Ephesus

Ephesus was wealthy and magnificent; it was especially known for its shrine to the Roman goddess Diana (whose Greek name was Artemis). Located on the west coast of Asia Minor, it not only was a major port, but it also was at the center of land routes to the most important cities of Asia Minor. Paul first visited this city about A.D. 52 during his second missionary journey and spent over two years there during his third missionary journey. After his release from his first imprisonment in Rome, Paul likely made several brief visits to Ephesus and left his close friend Timothy in charge of this church **(1 Timothy 1:3).** One of Paul's best-known letters is addressed to the Ephesians.

John went to Ephesus probably soon after the beginning of the Jewish revolt (A.D. 66). During the reign of Domitian (81–96), John was banished to Patmos where he received **Revelation.**

Read **Revelation 2:1–7.**

1. What qualities of Jesus are identified **(v. 1)?**

Omnipotense
Omnipresence

2. What good qualities were to be found in this congregation **(vv. 2–3, 6)?**

Hard Work
Perseverence
True Doctrine

3. For what does Jesus reprimand this church **(v. 4)?**

Stray from simple faith

4. What is the call to repentance **(v. 5)?**

Remember

5. What Gospel promise is given **(v. 7)?**

Tree of Life

6. What applications for today's church do you find in this message to the Ephesian Christians?

Smyrna

Located on an arm of the Aegean Sea, Smyrna rivaled Ephesus as a commercial city. Because of its beautiful setting, it boasted of being the "First

City of Asia in beauty and size." It sloped from the sea with its beautiful public buildings located on the rounded top of the hill Pagus. The westerly breeze kept it cool and comfortable throughout the year. The faithful support of Rome by the Smyrnians was proverbial.

Paul seems to have founded the church there during his third missionary journey (A.D. 53–57; see **Acts 19:10**). Possibly Polycarp, a pupil of John, was head of this church at this time. In A.D. 156, Roman authorities urged Polycarp to say, "Caesar is Lord." He refused with his famous statement, "Eighty and six years have I served Him, and He never did me any injury: how then can I blaspheme my King and my Savior?" Pressed further he finally expostulated, "You threaten me with fire that burns but for an hour, and after a little is extinguished, but are ignorant of the fire of the coming judgment and eternal punishment, reserved for the ungodly. But why delay? Bring forth what you will." Polycarp expressed in action Jesus' encouragement to Smyrna through John, "Be faithful, even to the point of death, and I will give you the crown of life" **(Revelation 2:10)**.

Read **Revelation 2:8–11.**

1. What does **verse 8** tell us about Jesus?

First & Last Resurrected

2. What good qualities were to be found here **(vv. 9–10)?**

Rich in faith despite afflictions

3. What special danger might these Christians have encountered in the day of persecution and affliction **(v. 10)?** Note that the 10-day persecution is symbolic for a complete or intense period of persecution.

prison, persecution

4. What words might have been an invitation to repentance?

Be not afraid
Be faithful

5. What is the special promise to these believers **(vv. 10–11)?**

Crown of Life

6. What applications to today's Christian would you make?

Be faithful to your beliefs

Pergamum

Because of its location on a huge rocky hill overlooking a great surrounding valley, the Romans made Pergamum the capital of the province Asia. Here the god of healing, Asclepius, was worshiped under the emblem of a serpent—for believers the very symbol of Satan. Many pagan altars, as well as the great altar to Zeus, were to be found here. As capital of the province, it was also a center for emperor worship with temples dedicated to Caesar. All Christians had to do to remain in good graces in society was to confess publicly, "Caesar is Lord," and offer a pinch of salt as a token of loyalty. Failure to do so meant loss of employment and social status, if not imprisonment and death. Some Christians reasoned, "What harm is there in doing that? We can still in our hearts worship Christ." They wanted to have it both ways—worship Christ in their hearts but worship Caesar in public.

Read **Revelation 2:12–17.**

1. What description of Jesus is given here **(v. 12)?**

Gives Law & Gospel

2. What word of commendation did Jesus have for this church **(v. 13)?**

Emperor worship

3. What word of reprimand did Jesus give **(vv. 14–15)?** For information about Balaam, refer to **Numbers 25:1–3; 31:16.**

4. What would happen if the people did not repent **(v. 16)?**

Law would devour

5. What is the promise **(v. 17)?**

Bread of Life

6. What applications for today do you find?

Thyatira

Situated in a valley connecting two other valleys, this city lacked natural fortifications and therefore was vulnerable to attack. The Romans maintained a strong military base in this city both to defend it and to obstruct the path of those who might seek to follow this easy route to attack the provincial capital, Pergamum. Thyatira was also a center of trade. In view of its character as an army post and a commercial city, vice and immorality were rampant—a constant temptation to the Christians who lived there.

Read **Revelation 2:18–29.**

1. How is Jesus described in **verse 18?**

2. What good things did Jesus say about this church **(v. 19)?**

3. What spiritual danger faced these people **(vv. 20–24)?**

4. What exhortation to repentance and what encouragement are found in **verses 20–24?**

5. What words of promise did Jesus offer **(vv. 26–29)?**

6. How might this message be applied to churches today?

Sardis

At one time this city had been the capital of Lydia, but it had fallen on hard times. The Romans helped it recover some of its former glory. In A.D. 17 it suffered a severe earthquake, but Tiberius helped the city rebuild.

Like Thyatira, it was famous for its woolen manufactures and its dyeing industry. The Roman system of roads secured for it the trade of central Asia.

Read **Revelation 3:1–6.**

1. What does **verse 1** say about Jesus?

2. What word of praise is to be found in this letter **(v. 4)?**

3. What condition did Jesus condemn in this church **(vv. 1–3)?**

4. With what words did Jesus call these people to repentance **(v. 3)?**

5. What is the word of promise **(vv. 4–5)?**

6. How might this message apply to Christians today?

Philadelphia

This city was founded by and named after Attalus II (whose devotion to his brother Eumenes gained for him the epithet "brother lover"). It was founded in 138 B.C. as a trade center for the rich volcanic region north of the city. Attalus founded Philadelphia as a center for the spread of the Greek language; therefore it had a certain "missionary" character from its beginning. It was subject to frequent earthquakes. It was a small city; so the congregation likely was quite small. Lying in a vine-growing region, the cult of Dionysus was predominant. Difficulties for Christians in this city seemed to have arisen more from Jewish opponents than from pagan adversaries.

Read **Revelation 3:7–13.**

1. How is Jesus described in **verse 7?**

2. What praise did Jesus have for this congregation **(vv. 8–10)?**

3. What danger might possibly have faced these Christians whom Jesus commended so highly?

4. How might **verse 11** be understood as a call to repentance?

5. What is the Gospel promise **(vv. 10–12)?**

6. What application for your Christian life and that of the entire church do you find in these words?

Laodicea

Located 40 miles southeast of Philadelphia, this city was founded in the third century before Christ by Antiochus II who named it in honor of his wife, Laodice. Under Roman rule it became a flourishing commercial center, noted for woolen carpets and clothing. It was a prosperous city, as is evident in **3:17–18.** This church was possibly established by Epaphras of Colossae **(Colossians 1:7; 4:12–13).** At the time of his first Roman imprisonment, Paul had not yet visited the Lycus valley **(Colossians 2:1)** but seems to have known some of the members by name **(Colossians 4:15)**.

Read **Revelation 3:14–22.**

1. What description of Jesus is offered in this letter **(v. 14)?**

2. What praise for this congregation, if any, do you find in this message?

3. What dangers surrounded the members of this church **(vv. 15–18)?**

4. What is the call to repentance **(vv. 18–19)?**

5. What is the Gospel **(vv. 20–21)?**

6. What applications to churches of our time do you find in this message to Laodicea?

For Next Time

Read **Revelation 4:1–5:14.**

Be faithful, even to the point of death, and I will give you the crown of life. Revelation 2:10

Lesson 3

Setting the Stage

Bible Basis
Revelation 4:1–5:14

Introduction
After preparing the readers of **Revelation 1–3** to receive the visions to come, John now in **chapters 4–5** describes the setting in which he received his revelation from Jesus and the angels.

Before the Throne of God
Read **Revelation 4.**

The voice of Jesus in **Revelation 1:10–11** invites John to write a scroll to be sent to the seven churches of Asia. Now that voice invites John to step into the court of God to receive the secret plan of God for the world and especially for His people **(4:1–2)**.

1. The Holy Spirit carried John before the very throne of God to receive God's revelation. More than 40 references to God's throne occur in **Revelation.** What does God's throne symbolize?

2. **Exodus 33:20** provides one possible explanation for why the radiance of God is described reflected in precious stones **(4:3)**. Explain.

3. The rainbow, reminiscent of God's promise to Noah, suggests that God in all His power and majesty is also the God of grace and mercy. The 24 elders seated on the 24 thrones surrounding the throne of God **(4:4)** represent the believers in every era of human history (the 12 tribes of

Israel to represent Old Testament believers and the 12 apostles to denote the believers of the New Testament era). The garments of white denote the righteousness of Christ with which His people are clothed. The gold crowns and the thrones symbolize their royal authority. Although the enthronement of the people of God lies in the future, believers in Jesus already have one foot in heaven. See **Philippians 3:20–4:1** and explain.

4. The flashes of lightning and peals of thunder, symbolic of the awesome authority, power, and glory of God remind one of God's revelation of Himself at Mount Sinai when He gave the Law to His people **(4:5)**. The seven lamps are the seven spirits of God and represent the Holy Spirit, who with His sevenfold gifts is active among the people of God to enlighten and endow them with heavenly wisdom **(Isaiah 11:1–2)**. (In His Law God condemns us, but by His Spirit through the Gospel He gives us eternal life and salvation.)

Commentators are not certain what the sea of glass represents. Some see it as a barrier that separates us from the throne of God **(4:6)**. Our sin prevents us from reaching up to Him. Through the Gospel of Jesus Christ, the Spirit reaches down to us to draw us to God and heaven.

Along with the 24 elders and the seven spirits, four living creatures are before the throne. These creatures are similar to those seen by Isaiah and Ezekiel. Read **Isaiah 6:1–7** and **Ezekiel 1; 10.** Then compare each of the following sets of references. Note the similarities between the vision of John and the visions of Isaiah and Ezekiel.

a. **Revelation 4:3** and **Ezekiel 1:28**

b. **Revelation 4:5** and **Ezekiel 1:13**

c. **Revelation 4:6** and **Ezekiel 1:5**

d. **Revelation 4:7** and **Ezekiel 1:10**

e. **Revelation 4:8** and **Ezekiel 1:18; 10:12**

f. **Revelation 4:8** and **Isaiah 6:2**

The Four Living Creatures

These living creatures seem to belong to a higher order of angels and are in the forefront of the hosts of angels who constantly worship God and serve creation. Equipped with many eyes, they are full of alertness and knowledge. They serve God and humankind with courage and strength (lion). They have patient steadfastness and strength which enables them to render service (ox). They are intelligent and wise (human face). They possess accurate swiftness, and they are eager to obey God and to serve (eagle).

The living creatures constantly praise God **(4:8)** as their Creator, especially for those attributes meaningful to God's people in time of persecution. He is *holy*—utterly separate from all created beings. He is *almighty*—able to protect and save His people. He is *eternal*—He alone is the source and basis of all that endures forever; He alone is utterly dependable.

Although the people of God (represented by the 24 elders) rule with Him, their authority is that delegated to them by God. The elders fall down in worship and cast down their golden crowns in homage to Him who possesses all power and authority in heaven and on earth (see **Matthew 28:18**).

An Unending Hymn of Praise

Take a closer look at the unending hymn of praise sung by the living creatures in **Revelation 4:8.** Recalling that the number *three* symbolizes God, note that the hymn has three lines and that each line has three elements—three holies, three titles for God, and three attributes of God.

1. Compare this hymn to that sung by the seraphim in **Isaiah 6:3.** What

does the triple "holy" indicate?

The similarities in both songs of the titles for God is evident in some English translations. The Hebrew of **Isaiah 6:3** literally reads *Yahweh Sabaoth.* Some English versions translate this quite literally as "LORD of hosts." This emphasizes God as the commander of the angelic armies. Others translate the phrase as LORD Almighty. The Septuagint (the Greek translation of the Old Testament used by many early Christians) regularly translates *Yahweh Sabaoth* as Lord Almighty, the same phrase used here in Revelation. Both *Lord Almighty* and *Lord of hosts* reflect the majesty and power of God.

2. Now look at the hymn sung by the 24 elders in **Revelation 4:11.** For what do they praise God?

3. Why is our recognition of God as the Creator of all things so essential for our understanding of the Gospel of Jesus Christ?

The Bible in Revelation

John could use symbolic language and verbal allusions because his readers understood them and could make the proper applications. Compare at least three of the sets of references below. Then make a statement about the relationship between the Old and New Testaments.

1. **Revelation 4:1; Ezekiel 1:1; Mark 1:10; John 1:51**

2. **Revelation 4:1; 1 Kings 22:18–19; Amos 3:7; Jeremiah 23:18**

3. **Revelation 4:2; Isaiah 6:1; 66:1; Psalm 47:8**

4. **Revelation 4:3; Ezekiel 1:26–28; Psalm 104:2; Genesis 9:16–17**

5. **Revelation 4:5; Exodus 19:16–19; Psalm 18:6–13**

Who Is Worthy to Open the Scroll?

Read **Revelation 5:1–5.**

What is the scroll? Several theories have been advanced.

Some identify the scroll with the Lamb's Book of Life (see **Revelation 3:5; 13:8; 17:8; 20:12, 15; 21:27**). Names were written on both sides (writing on the reverse side of papyrus was very difficult) because of the great multitude of the people of God.

Others believe that the scroll is the Old Testament. Here Jesus takes the scroll of prophecy and declares, as He did in Nazareth, "Today this scripture is fulfilled in your hearing" **(Luke 4:21).**

However, the most satisfactory understanding is that the scroll contains the revelation of those events that John was to communicate. The scroll records God's redemptive plan from Christ's ministry on earth to the plan's triumphal climax in the culmination of this age when a new heaven and a new earth will be established. The scroll was completely sealed (with seven seals) to indicate that it could only be opened by one worthy to do so. No creature was found worthy to open this scroll or even peek inside to see what the future held. Thus John wept.

An elder comforted John by pointing him to the one who was worthy. The elder used two messianic terms familiar to those versed in the Old Testament—the Lion of the tribe of Judah **(Genesis 49:9–10)** and the Root of David **(Isaiah 11:1–10).**

"Worthy Is the Lamb"

Read **Revelation 5:6–14.** Here John is shown what the ascension and enthronement of Jesus looked like in heaven.

The Lion of the tribe of Judah is now pictured as a Lamb. These two descriptions illustrate the striking, unique combination of majesty and humility that characterizes the life of Jesus.

1. How is the Lamb described in the first part of **verse 6?** What is the significance of Jesus being described in this way (see **Isaiah 53:4–7**)?

2. In the Old Testament, horns symbolize strength **(Deuteronomy 33:17)** and political power **(Daniel 7:24).** What does it mean that Jesus has seven horns?

3. What do the seven eyes symbolize?

The Lamb takes the scroll from the hand of God. This symbolizes not only that the Lamb can open the scroll, but that He controls the events recorded there and uses them for the furthering of God's kingdom.

After the Lamb takes the scroll, the four living creatures and the 24 elders break into song. Note that this is a new song occasioned by what the Lamb has brought about.

4. According to their song, why is the Lamb worthy and what has He brought about?

5. The voices of a great number of angels then join the chorus of praise. What is the content of their song?

6. Why would the great multitudes of angels already confirmed in their eternal bliss be so concerned and joyful about a redemption that pertains to human beings? Before responding, read **1 Peter 1:10–12; Luke 15:10;** and **Hebrews 1:14.**

7. At this point John's vision anticipates the end of time when every creature everywhere will join the song of praise. Why would all created things join the human family in this hymn of praise for the Lamb's great work of redemption? (See **Colossians 1:20** and **Romans 8:18–22.**)

8. To whom is this praise directed? What does this say about the nature of Jesus?

Even as they began this great hymn of praise in **4:8,** so the four living creatures also bring it to an end in **5:14.**

For Reflection

✔ 1. As the Holy Spirit works in the lives of God's people, when do we stand in awe of God's created universe and Christ's redemptive work as did the four creatures and the 24 elders?

2. How might acquiring a greater understanding of and appreciation for God's great works of creation and redemption affect the way we relate to others?

For Next Time

Read **Revelation 6:1–7:17.**

You are worthy to take the scroll and to open its seals, because You were slain, and with Your blood You purchased men for God from every tribe and language and people and nation. You have made them to be a kingdom and priests to serve our God, and they will reign on the earth. Revelation 5:9–10

Lesson 4

The First Cycle of Tribulations: The Seven Seals

Bible Basis

Revelation 6:1–7:17

Introduction

We now are ready to receive the first cycle of revelations of those tribulations that are to occur. In **Revelation** we have three cycles, but each covers the same ground from different perspectives and with different symbols. The first cycle comes in the form of seals **(6:1–7:17)**, the second in the form of trumpet blasts **(8:6–11:19)**, and the third in the form of plagues and bowls of God's wrath **(15:1–16:21)**.

In addition, twice we will witness the cosmic struggle between Christ and His saints against Satan and all his evil hosts. The first struggle, or grand sweeping view of all things, is described in **Revelation 12:1–14:20** and the second in **Revelation 20:1–10**.

Each of these cycles and both of these grand sweeping views tells us something about what will occur throughout the New Testament era and something about what will occur at the end of history. The first cycle deals with tribulations among humankind.

The Four Horsemen

Some of the earliest Christians mistakenly believed that Christ would return within their lifetime to right all injustices and to usher in the new age. On the contrary, many grim events occurred to shake one's belief in the reign of Christ. A series of destructive earthquakes shook the world around A.D. 60. The seemingly invincible Roman armies suffered a humiliating defeat by the Parthians two years later.

After fire destroyed Rome in A.D. 64, the Christians were blamed for the catastrophe and were cruelly persecuted. Then after four years of violent bloodshed, the great city of Jerusalem was destroyed in A.D. 70. After Nero's suicide in A.D. 68, the empire suffered from political chaos for a whole year as four different people fought to become emperor. Then in A.D. 79, Mount Vesuvius erupted. It covered the luxury seashore cities of Pompeii, Herculaneum, and Stabiae with debris more than 60 feet deep. In A.D. 92 the empire suffered from a serious grain shortage.

Then, as now, in the midst of all these catastrophes people asked, "Where is your gracious God?" Christians themselves questioned the reign of the living Christ—especially when they endured suffering because of their allegiance to Him. To bolster their trust in the providence, protection, and rule of Christ, John received this first cycle of visions to share with God's people on earth.

Read **Revelation 6:1–8.**

There are differing interpretations as to what the white horse represents. Because of the color of the horse, some identify the rider with Christ (see **19:11**) or see this as symbolic for the conquest of the Gospel as it is preached throughout the world. But in the context of the other horsemen, it is perhaps best understood as sinful people's conquering spirit, lust for power, and desire to tyrannize other people.

1. What does the red horse and its rider symbolize?

2. What does the black horse and its rider symbolize?

3. What does the pale horse and its rider symbolize?

4. What examples of situations created by each of these four horsemen can you adduce from recent history? from your own life today?

5. Why would a gracious God permit people to endure all of the suffering created by these catastrophes?

The Fifth Seal

Read **Revelation 6:9–11.**
1. Who is it that John sees under the altar **(v. 9)**?

2. Why are these souls crying to be vindicated?

3. What response do the souls receive **(v. 11)**? Of what does this assure them?

The Great Earthquake

Read **Revelation 6:12–17.**
Suffering and martyrdom will not continue forever. Eventually this age with its evil and death must come to an end, and a new age will dawn. Upheavals in nature point to the great day of the Lord. Through such upheavals God is present and active in judgment to overthrow the results of human arrogance. Upheavals in nature are foretastes of the final judgment of God on all human pride and rebellion. No one will escape; the entire fabric of society will be affected **(6:15).** Thus in the sixth seal John sees the end of this world.
1. This section is built on biblical allusions with which the original read-

ers would have been well acquainted. Look up the following Bible passages and note how the end of the world is described in each. Note also the similarities with this section of **Revelation.**

a. **Isaiah 2:12–22**

b. **Isaiah 24:1–23**

c. **Isaiah 34:2–4**

2. Compare Jesus' description of the last days in **Luke 21:8–19, 25–36** with this and the previous two sections.

3. What does Jesus say will happen at the time the great upheavals in nature take place (**v. 27;** see also **Mark 13:26–27**)?

4. With what attitude are Christians to prepare for this time (**Luke 21:36**)?

The Sealing of the 144,000

In John's vision, the seventh seal is yet to be opened. **Revelation 8:1,** the opening of the seventh seal, introduces the next cycle, which depicts the same time period from another perspective. But before John receives that vision, there is an interlude. That interlude shows John what happens to the people of God in the midst of the suffering the world must endure. Read **Revelation 7:1–8.**

Four angels of God hold back the four winds of destruction that would ravish the earth and its inhabitants. (The "four corners of the earth" denote the entire world.)

The 144,000 have been sealed to keep them secure in their faith in spite of all evil in the world. They represent all believers in every period of human history (12 for the Old Testament tribes of Israel × 12 for the New Testament apostles × 1,000 for the number of completeness). The sealing does not protect them from physical sufferings or death, but it does ensure their glorious entrance into heaven.

The 144,000 are not only those martyrs who were killed in defense of the Gospel; they include all believers. Every Christian in one way or another is a martyr; we all give witness to the faith that is within us, and we all are tested in various ways. Not only can we be sure that we will be tested, but we can also be certain that God will keep us secure until we have attained our goal.

What assurance do each of the following passages provide that God will keep you secure unto heaven, even in times of tribulation?

1. **Philippians 1:6**

2. **1 Corinthians 1:4–9**

3. **2 Thessalonians 3:1–3**

4. **1 Thessalonians 5:23–24**

5. **John 10:27–30**

6. **1 Peter 1:3–5**

7. **Romans 8:26–39**

8. **Jude 24–25**

The Song of Victory

In the first eight verses of **chapter 7** John has described the *church militant*—the people of God in this world as they struggle against the forces of evil in the power of the Spirit of God. Now, in **verses 9–17,** he describes the *church triumphant*—the people of God who during their lifetime triumphed over the forces of Satan and are forever with God in bliss.

Read **Revelation 7:9–17.**

1. How is God's promise to Abraham **(Genesis 15:5)** fulfilled in this company before the throne?

2. What is the significance of the white robes and palms (see **Revelation 7:14; John 12:12–13**)?

3. What similarities do you note between **Revelation 7:10, 12** and **Psalm 98**?

4. What blessings can you anticipate as you look forward to your reception into the company of those before the throne of the Lamb **(7:14–17)**?

For Next Time
Read **Revelation 8:1–9:21.**

For the Lamb at the center of the throne will be their shepherd; He will lead them to springs of living water. And God will wipe away every tear from their eyes. Revelation 7:17

Lesson 5

The Second Cycle of Tribulations: The Seven Trumpets

Bible Basis

Revelation 8:1–9:21

Introduction

An old adage, "repetition is the mother of study," emphasizes the importance both of frequent review and of the value of describing a subject in many different ways. At times the way a matter is presented to us will determine whether or not we'll understand it. So, in describing to John events that will occur during the time period between Christ's coming and the Last Day, the Spirit of God used a variety of revelations and symbols.

The first cycle as described in **Revelation 6** focuses on evils and tribulations caused by human sin. We might call this people's inhumanity to others. But in **Revelation 7,** the Lord assures His people of every generation that He will preserve them in the midst of affliction and persecution. In the age to come they will stand before the throne of God in eternal bliss.

The second cycle **(Revelation 8:6–9:21,** introduced by **Revelation 8:1–5)** focuses on the evils in nature that cause people to suffer. Not only human sin, but also Satan's forces from hell affect nature and cause human suffering. Yet in the midst of this intense suffering, the people of God continue to witness triumphantly to the grace and glory of God in Jesus Christ, who lived, died, and rose again to earn our freedom from sin, death, and all evil.

Preparation for the Second Cycle

Read **Revelation 8:1–5.** The opening of the seventh seal both concludes the first cycle and introduces the second cycle. After the interlude described in **Revelation 7,** Jesus the Lamb broke the seventh seal. At first nothing happened; there was "silence in heaven for about half an hour" **(8:1).** According to rabbinic theology, silence preceded great acts of God's revelation and judgment (see the apocryphal books 2 Esdras 6:39 and Wisdom 18:14–15).

This was the prelude to the blowing of the seven trumpets announcing God's judgment upon the earth (the number *seven* indicates the *totality* of God's judgment). But just as the seals could not be broken until someone was found who was worthy to break them, so the trumpets could not sound until the prayers of God's people reached heaven.

1. What does this imagery suggest about the place of prayer in the reign of Jesus until the Last Day?

2. In Old Testament times, the trumpet was sounded, among other things, to warn people of danger and to call them together in assembly. Read **Joel 2:1–2, 11.** What does the trumpet herald? Read **Joel 2:12–17.** What can the people do?

Nature Polluted

Even as the four horsemen depict evils in human relationships that result from sin, so the first four trumpet blasts portray the evils in the natural universe that come from human sin and demonic activity. Read **Revelation 8:6–13.**

1. As you begin your study of the plagues in nature produced by the sounding of the first four trumpets, look up **Romans 8:19–22.** What relationship did Paul see between sin and phenomena in nature? What hope for this natural universe did he hold?

2. The first plague **(8:7)** points to the evil results of sin on land. The second **(8:8–9)** notes catastrophes caused by sin on the seas. The third

speaks of the pollution of fresh water **(8:10–11)**. The fourth plague affects our sources of light **(8:12)**. Identify recent events that point to the occurrence of such events today.

3. According to **Joel 2:30–32** and **Acts 2:18–21,** what interpretation are we to give to catastrophic events in nature we observe today? Where can people turn for salvation?

4. What significance is there in that only a fraction of nature is consumed by these events **(8:7–12;** see also **Zechariah 13:7–9)?**

5. Why don't the people of God have anything to fear from these events (see **Psalm 46:1–3**)?

6. The fourth plague brings darkness. What does darkness symbolize in **Amos 5:18–20; Joel 2:1–2; Mark 13:24–26; Isaiah 13:9–13?** What is the meaning of darkness in **Colossians 1:13?**

7. Look up the following passages. What similarity do you find between the plagues of **Revelation** and those of Egypt?
   a. **Exodus 9:13–35/Revelation 8:7**

b. **Exodus 7:14–24/Revelation 8:8–9**

c. **Exodus 10:21–29/Revelation 8:12**

8. What significance is there in the similarity between the 10 plagues in Egypt and the subsequent Exodus and that of the plagues in **Revelation** and the Last Day (see **Revelation 1:5–7; 15:1–4; Luke 21:25–28**)?

The Assault from the Abyss (The First Woe)

In the transitional verse **Revelation 8:13,** an eagle or vulture (a symbol of impending destruction and doom, see **Luke 17:37; Hosea 8:1**) announces even greater woes to befall unbelievers. (The phrase "inhabitants of the earth" is used in **Revelation** to refer to humanity in hostility to God.) At the sound of the fifth trumpet, John sees the fallen star (probably Satan) given the key to the abyss. Although God does not cause evil, He permits the fallen angels and humankind to experience the results of their sinful actions.

This vision in **Revelation 9:1–21** presupposes a close connection between two worlds, both of which God created at the beginning—the world of the spirit as well as the material universe **(Genesis 1:1; Colossians 1:16).** The demons were also created by God, originally as angels, but in the exercise of their free will they chose to rebel against their Creator and to seek the destruction of all that is good—including the world with its human inhabitants.

Read **Revelation 9:1–12.** Here John views the growing intensity of the warfare between Satan and his followers against humankind, the creation of God. The abyss is hell as well as the accummulation of evil, to which all people contribute, and by which all people, whether they choose it or not, are affected.

The locusts, which again remind us of the plagues of Egypt that preceded the exodus of God's Old Testament people, will be let loose on earth prior to the final exodus of all of God's people into the new age. These are the demons who injure people rather than vegetation. Their sting is extremely painful (like scorpions). They are extremely intelligent and cunning (human faces), are very destructive (lions' teeth), are well protected (breastplates of iron), and have as their king one whose name means "destroyer" (possibly Satan himself).

However, their power and the duration of their assault upon humankind are limited. This is not yet the final assault of Satan on humankind, in particular the Christians. God permits the harm to come only to those who do "not have the seal of God on their foreheads" (**9:4**; unbelievers). Moreover, these minions from hell "were not given power to kill them, but only to torture them for five months" (**9:5**). God limits the effects and duration of this onslaught so that people might see in their suffering the judgment of God on their sin and hear in this trumpet blast the merciful voice of God calling them to repentance and saving faith.

It is possible that this trumpet blast and the next herald the unleashing of false teachings with all of their destructive power and their ability to torment people in mind and soul and sometimes body. Jesus warns us that false prophets will appear and deceive many people (**Matthew 24:10–11**). That may be how these hordes from hell wreak their destruction.

The Reserves Are Brought In (The Second Woe)

Read **Revelation 9:13–21**. At the sound of the sixth trumpet a cavalry comes to reinforce these demonic enemies of God and humankind. The four angels of destruction who previously had been restrained for just this time are let loose upon the enemies of God's people on earth. The fact that the voice came "from the horns of the golden altar" (**9:13**) suggests that the prayers of God's people have a part to play in this drama. (On this golden altar the angel had offered the prayers of the saints to God [**8:3**].)

Although the conflict is intensified, again only a portion of humanity is destroyed. This indicates that the era of God's grace is not yet exhausted. **Revelation 9:20–21** suggests God's gracious will and purpose in permitting these woes to befall humankind. Humanity's great sin is that of idolatry—worship of self and whatever people themselves produce and do (humanism can be one aspect of this self-worship). This idolatry strengthens the destructive work of the demonic spirits in the world and bears fruit in murders, magic arts, sexual immorality, and thefts (**9:21**).

One of God's purposes in permitting these evils from the satanic forces to occur is to lead unbelievers to repentance and to a saving knowledge of and faith in Jesus Christ, the Savior **(9:21).** However, these verses also indicate that we are not to expect many to repent. In fact most will continue on their rebellious path against God.

1. What evidences do you see that God has not yet withdrawn His offer of grace, forgiveness, and acceptance from this world?

2. What does all this suggest about why God has placed you in this world at this time and place?

For Next Time
Read **Revelation 10:1–11:19.**

Another angel, who had a golden censer, came and stood at the altar. He was given much incense to offer, with the prayers of all the saints, on the golden altar before the throne. The smoke of the incense, together with the prayers of the saints, went up before God from the angel's hand. Revelation 8:3–4

Lesson 6

"What's a Nice Person Like You Doing in This Kind of World?"

Bible Basis
Revelation 10:1–11:19

Introduction

Recall that **Revelation 7** was an interlude between the sixth and seventh seals and pictured the church, militant and triumphant. Now we come to an interlude between the sixth and seventh trumpet blasts. This interlude also deals with the church—this time with the church and its mission and final destiny.

One mystery that puzzles many people is this: Why, with the world so evil, does the good God leave His chosen people on earth to suffer affliction at the hands of the enemies of Christ?

In their distress God's people cry out, "How long, Sovereign Lord, holy and true, until You judge the inhabitants of the earth and avenge our blood?" **(Revelation 6:10)**. They pray, "Amen. Come, Lord Jesus" **(22:20)**. Yet the Lord tarries, and His people continue to suffer. For what purpose does He place His people in this world of evil and death and then delay His coming to deliver them?

The visions recorded in **Revelation 10** and **11** uncover some of this mystery for us.

The One Who Calls Us
Read **Revelation 10:1–6.**

Whether or not we fulfill the responsibilities given us often depends on who gives us those responsibilities. In this vision John sees a "mighty angel" holding a little scroll lying open in his hand. **Revelation 10:1–11** suggests that God's people are placed in this world to achieve specific God-given responsibilities. In this section we are given clues to help us identify the angel and the importance of our mission.

1. Previous to this whom has John seen whose face is like the sun **(Matthew 17:1–2; Revelation 1:16)?**

2. What might the rainbow point to **(Genesis 9:12–17)?**

3. Of what would the cloud and legs like fiery pillars remind John's readers **(Exodus 13:21–22; 14:19, 24; 40:34–38)?**

4. What do clouds symbolize in these passages: **Zephaniah 1:15; Psalm 97:2; Daniel 7:13; Matthew 24:30**?

5. Who might this angel be?

6. What significance is there in that this giant plants his right foot on the sea and his left foot on the land?

The Purpose and Task for Which We Are Called

Read **Revelation 10:5–7.** The mighty angel solemnly swears that our years of waiting are over; this age is coming to a close, and the new age is about to dawn. With the blast of the seventh trumpet all that God purposed in His creation, made possible by the blood of the Lamb **(Revelation 5:9–10)**, will be brought to fulfillment.

We would expect the end to come immediately after **Revelation 10:7,** but the trumpet is not actually blown until **Revelation 11:15.** The intervening material between **10:7** and **11:15** seems to be an intrusion. But not so.

In the previous revelations concerning the first six trumpets, the vision focused on the evil and misery that will flourish in the world during the New Testament age until the Last Day. Now we are to focus on this period from a different perspective—that of the people of God and their activity in the world. While the focus before was on Satan and the mischievous work of his followers, now the emphasis is on God's activity of divine grace through His people on earth.

Read **Revelation 10:8–11.**

1. Compare this section with **Ezekiel 2:8–3:4.** What is Ezekiel commissioned to do? (Note that a more correct translation of **Rev. 10:11** is ". . . prophesy again *before* many peoples.")

2. In what sense is this the commission of the whole church (see **Matthew 28:19–20**)?

3. What is the meaning of the command to "take and eat" the little scroll?

4. What is the significance of the scroll being both sweet and sour (see **Psalm 119:103; Jeremiah 15:16; Ezekiel 3:3**)?

5. Why is this mission so urgent **(10:7)?**

6. According to **Matthew 24:14,** what will happen before the end of this age?

7. What opportunities do you have today to fulfill your part in this mission of God's people?

Confidence to Confess Boldly

Reflect on your experiences in confessing your faith before other people. What incidences can you recall when speaking of your faith was easy? When was it difficult? When, if ever, did you meet with outright hostility?

The vision of the two witnesses **(11:1–13)** was given to encourage you especially when you meet with ridicule, hostility, and persecution as you profess your faith and life in Christ.

Read **Revelation 11:1–6.** John was commanded to measure the temple. This alludes to a vision Ezekiel had 14 years after the destruction of Solomon's temple in which the prophet watched as a man measured the heavenly temple and the glory of the Lord returned **(Ezekiel 40–43).** Ezekiel was to relay his vision to his fellow exiles to comfort them with the knowledge that God would rebuild His temple. Because this was an ideal temple, Ezekiel's vision was no doubt a prophecy not only of the rebuilding of the physical temple but of the building of the Christian church as well.

The temple in John's vision represents the true church, that is, all believers (see **1 Corinthians 3:16–17; 2 Corinthians 6:16; Ephesians 2:19–22**). The measuring of the temple indicates that these believers will be protected by God even as He permits unbelievers to have some power to attack the church ("trample on the holy city"). This will occur throughout the New Testament era ("42 months"; see below). Although the saints will suffer and even be killed, they will not lose their faith and perish in unbelief.

However, the outer court (the Court of the Gentiles in the Jerusalem temple) was not to be measured (i.e., protected). This represents either the unbelieving pagan world or, possibly, believers who compromise their faith.

The 42 months represent the Gospel age—the period of time from Christ's ministry on earth to the Last Day. 42 months x 30 days per month = 1,260 days, or 3 1/2 years ("a time, times and half a time" in **Revelation 12:14**). This will be a period not only of Gospel proclamation but also of affliction. This time span symbolizes a limited period of time during which evil is allowed free rein. (See **Daniel 7:25; 12:7, 11**).

Throughout this age the two witnesses will continue to proclaim the Gospel of Christ. The two witnesses refer to all Christian witnesses; *two* possibly alludes to the disciples who went out two by two to witness **(Luke 10:1)**. Or it may indicate the relatively small number of witnesses in relation to the rest of the world. The sackcloth may denote the message of repentance that Christ's witnesses believe and also proclaim so that people will come to faith in their Savior, Jesus Christ. Or the sackcloth may be symbolic of the suffering and mourning these witnesses will experience.

The two lampstands and the two olive trees refer to a vision the Old Testament prophet Zechariah saw. They symbolize the royal house of Zerubbabel (who led the people after they returned from exile) and the anointed priesthood, both empowered by the Holy Spirit (see **Zechariah 4**). The lampstands and the olive trees indicate that the whole community of God's redeemed people during this age comprise a royal house of priests to our God and Father (see **1 Peter 2:5, 9; Revelation 1:6; 5:10**).

The Word of God proclaimed by His faithful witnesses is one of life or death; "fire comes from their mouths and devours their enemies" (**Revelation 11:5;** see also **Matthew 16:19; 18:18–20; John 20:21–23**). It is the Word of Christ that will be the standard of judgment at the Last Day; those who reject the Gospel thereby bring upon themselves their own condemnation (see **John 12:48**).

Revelation 11:5–6 alludes to power given to Elijah **(1 Kings 17:1; 2 Kings 1:10–11)** and Moses **(Exodus 7:14–21)**. Even as God raised up Moses and Elijah to be His witnesses in their respective generations, so in every generation He raises up faithful witnesses to proclaim His message. Even as He empowered Moses and Elijah to perform great marvels in order to accomplish their mission, so He gives His people today power and protection to fulfill their purpose as Christians in an unbelieving world **(Revelation 11:6)**. As surely as Jesus has come to earth to live, die, and rise again to pay for the sins of the world, He empowers us to witness with boldness and confidence the Good News of the salvation He freely offers.

The Church's Final Persecution and Triumph

God has never promised that being and living as a member of His family will be easy in this present age. On the contrary, we can be sure that as Christians we will be called to suffer for our faith in one form or another **(John 16:33)**. Although throughout history the people of God have enjoyed periods of relative calm and success, these periods have alternated with seasons of intense persecution. For example, the early Jerusalem Christians initially were severely persecuted **(Acts 8:1)**. This period was followed by a season of relative peace and acceptance **(Acts 9:31)**. What examples from more recent history can you suggest?

These cycles of persecution and calm will continue until the end, with each cycle foreshadowing the final persecution of the church and its final triumph. Read **Revelation 11:7–14**. In symbolic language, this section shows us that final persecution and triumph in which the church follows its Lord to death and resurrection.

1. When will this persecution take place (**v. 7**; see also **Matthew 24:14**)?

2. Who is the beast and from where does he come (see **Revelation 20:1–3**)?

3. What does the beast do to the witnesses (i.e., the church)?

4. What does Sodom symbolize **(Genesis 18:20–21)**? Egypt **(Exodus 5:1–9)**? Together with the reference to Jerusalem, which crucified its Lord, what do these places symbolize?

5. What is significant about the fact that people from all over the world gaze on the bodies of witnesses and refuse them burial?

6. Why do the inhabitants of the earth (unbelievers) celebrate the church's death?

7. Three and a half days symbolize a short, evil period of time (probably equivalent to the "short time" of **Revelation 20:3**). What happens after three and a half days? Compare this to **Ezekiel 37:1–14.**

8. Why are those who see the church come to life terrified?

Following their being brought back to life, the witnesses are called up to heaven and the inhabitants of the earth begin to experience God's judgment and have no choice but to acknowledge Him as God of all. But this is only the beginning of the judgment they will experience. As **Revelation 11:14** tells us the second woe is past and the third is soon to follow (that occurs in the next section).

The Day of Triumph

Read **Revelation 11:15–19.** The blowing of the trumpet by the seventh angel introduces the Last Day—a day of triumph for all believers, but a day of judgment and condemnation for all who rejected the mercy of God in Christ (the third woe). The heavenly host declare the triumphal reign of the Lord and His Christ **(v. 15)**. God has always reigned, but now all His enemies are subdued and He reigns eternally without opposition.

The elders, symbolizing God's people of all eras, join in the hymn of thanksgiving to Him who has entered His eternal reign, a reign established by a great demonstration of divine wrath against the defiant anger and hostility of the world **(vv. 16–18)**.

The cosmic disturbances **(v. 19)** all point to God's just and righteous judgment on His enemies, all the persons and forces of evil and unbelief. But for believers there is an eternal reward **(v. 18)** and complete access to the presence of God (symbolized by the ark of the covenant **[v. 19]**). In the Old Testament the ark was the place where God localized His presence among His people. But because of their sin access to the ark was severely restricted. The high priest could enter the Most Holy Place where it was kept only once a year.

At this point the book of **Revelation** might be concluded. But there is more that God wants to reveal. John now in **Revelation 12:1–14:20** will proceed to explain the underlying causes for all the hostility, opposition, and persecution of God's people on earth.

For Next Time

Read **Revelation 12:1–14:20,** giving special attention to **chapter 12.**

We give thanks to You, Lord God Almighty, the One who is and who was, because You have taken Your great power and have begun to reign. Revelation 11:17

Lesson 7

The Gathering Storm

Bible Basis

Revelation 12:1–17

Introduction

Each of the previous cycles in the book of **Revelation** covers the period between the time of Christ and the Last Day. This was true of the vision of the seven seals **(6:1–8:5)** and of the blowing of the seven trumpets **(8:6–11:19)**. This time frame is also the subject of the first grand sweeping view recorded in **12:1–14:20.**

This overview marks the introduction of the second division of this book. It stands between the first two cycles (the seven seals and the seven trumpets) and the remainder of the book. The first 11 chapters form a whole in themselves—after which the book might well have ended.

In **Revelation 12:1** the author makes a fresh beginning. Although the theme of the second division is the same as that of the first, the writer pursues new regions of thought and uses symbolic figures that are almost wholly new.

In the first part of **Revelation** John pictures the outward struggle between the church and the world. Now, in these next chapters, the underlying cause of this hostility is revealed. It is the age-long conflict between God and Satan that accounts for the persecution that the church experiences. Through His life, suffering, death, and resurrection Christ won the crucial battle in behalf of all His people. But the devil still does not give up; he continues his struggle to enslave and destroy all of God's creatures and creation. All history from the victorious work of Christ on earth to the Last Day is the violent death struggle between the church and Satan, with God and Christ behind the church.

The actors who play the major roles in this cosmic struggle are introduced in **Revelation 12–14.** Then, in **chapters 15–20,** John depicts God's coming in judgment to destroy His enemies once for all. Finally, in **chapters 21–22** he describes the eternal future that awaits all the faithful people of God.

Dragon, Woman, and Child

Chapter 12 is really quite fascinating. It is the story of a mother and her child hotly pursued by a vicious dragon. Read **Revelation 12:1–6.**

To understand this scene, one must be acquainted with its rich symbolism.

1. *Sign* is a word used to denote those great spectacles that occur in human history to point to the consummation of this age. What signs did Jesus tell us would precede the Last Day **(Luke 21:11, 25; Acts 2:19)?**

2. Although the child represents the Messiah, the woman who bears the child does not stand for Mary. Rather, before giving birth to the child, the woman symbolizes the people of Israel, God's Old Testament church. After the child is born, the woman symbolizes the believers of the New Testament. Explain.

3. Note how the woman is adorned **(12:1).** Her garment of the sun denotes glory and exaltation. That the moon is under her feet indicates that the woman exercises dominion. The crown is a symbol of royalty. Remember that the number 12 symbolizes either the people of God in the Old Testament or in the New; the number 24 stands for both together. Here the 12 stars indicate the Old Testament people of God from whom the child was born. After the birth of the child, the woman symbolizes the church.

That this sign appeared in heaven indicates that this is how God from the perspective of eternity views His people. What does this description suggest about the worth of the people of God of both Old and New Testament eras? How does this differ from the picture that we might have given only a temporal, earthly perspective?

4. The second person in this scene is the child who is to be born (12:2, 5). This is a clear reference to such passages as **Genesis 3:15; Isaiah 7:14; 9:6; Psalm 2:9; Galatians 4:4–5.** What do these passages tell you about this child?

5. In **Revelation 12:3** another being appears—"an enormous red dragon with seven heads and ten horns and seven crowns on his heads."

Red indicates blood, symbolic of the destruction that the dragon accomplishes in the world. The word *crowns* in **12:3** is a different word in Greek than the one used in **verse 1.** The type of crown in **verse 3** (*diadēma*) denotes the kind worn by Persian kings and indicates that the wearer claims to be God. Thus the seven crowned heads point to the dominion that the dragon deceptively wields over the world; however, this is abrogated authority that does not belong to him naturally. It belongs only to God, to Jesus Christ. The 10 horns denote his claim to have power over all aspects of life. According to **Revelation 12:9** and **20:2,** who is this dragon?

6. The stage is set; the players have been identified. Let us proceed to the drama. This conflict between the dragon and God and His creatures began already in eternity. When God created the heavens (Genesis 1:1), all of His heavenly creatures were good (see **Job 38:4–7**). In His love God gave all of His rational creatures a free will. He did not want the angels or human beings to be robots who loved and trusted in Him because they had no alternative. He gave these beings the freedom to choose.

Not content with being creatures of God, certain angels wanted to be as God. They rebelled against Him to establish their own independence. Since then they have sought to crush the power of God by destroying His creation. Some scholars believe that **verse 4,** which speaks of the sweeping of a third of the stars out of heaven, is an allusion to this rebellion in the heavenly realm, a rebellion that has its counterpart on earth among humankind. In such an interpretation the third of the stars could indicate the proportion of angels that the dragon took with him in his rebellion against God. What do the following passages indicate about this rebellion in heaven and its consequences?

a. **2 Peter 2:4**

b. **Ephesians 6:12**

c. **Jude 6**

d. **John 8:44**

e. **1 John 3:8**

Already in Eden the serpent sought to destroy humankind by inducing Adam and Eve to seek to be as God through independence from God **(Genesis 3:1–5).** In His grace God promised a Savior, the offspring of the woman who would crush Satan **(Genesis 3:15).** In the years following, the people of God yearned for this Redeemer. Their long centuries of eager, even painful, waiting were like that of a pregnant woman **(Revela-**

tion **12:2**). But Satan constantly stood before the people of God (the woman) intending to "devour her child the moment it was born" **(12:4).**

In God's time Israel through Mary brought forth the Savior "who will rule all the nations with an iron scepter" **(Revelation 12:5).** This is an obvious reference to **Psalm 2:6–9,** a coronation psalm that exalts the Messiah and His everlasting rule over all things.

In Jesus' infancy, Satan used Herod in his attempt to destroy the Savior so that he might frustrate God's plan of salvation and thus destroy all humankind. Throughout His ministry Jesus encountered Satan and his temptations designed to deter Jesus from His saving mission. Even Jesus' miracles were part of this struggle between God and Satan.

7. At the successful conclusion of His saving mission, Jesus in triumph ascended into heaven beyond any further satanic designs **(12:5).** But the woman (now representing God's New Testament people, the church) continues to live in this world subject to Satan's temptations. However, God has prepared a refuge (the desert, **v. 6**) for her. This stay in the desert lasts for 1,260 days, or "a time, times and half a time" **(Daniel 7:25; Revelation 12:14).** This is the period of the present age during which the people of God, surrounded by God's enemies, witness to salvation in Jesus.

What memories would this reference to the desert as a place of refuge bring to John's readers? See the passages below for clues.

- **Exodus 16:1–10,** especially **v. 10**

- **Deuteronomy 8:2–5**

- **1 Kings 17:2–6**

- **1 Kings 19:2–9**

- **Matthew 2:13–15**

- **Hosea 2:14–15**

8. What assurances of safety do God's people have in the desert refuge provided for them in this world?
- **1 John 1:3**

- **2 Corinthians 13:11–14**

What do these passages suggest about a primary purpose of congregational life? of the importance of active involvement in a congregation of believers throughout life?

War in Heaven

Read **Revelation 12:7–12.** This conflict in heaven is not Satan's original rebellion and fall at the dawn of this created universe. Rather, it seems to be the result of the completion of Christ's saving work. It appears that before then Satan had been free to enter the heavenly precincts to lodge accusations against God's people. Indeed, the word *Satan* means "accuser."

1. What notable examples of Satan accusing the people of God do we have in the Old Testament (see **Job 1:6–12** and **Zechariah 3:1–5**)?

When Christ died on the cross and rose again in our place, Satan was cast out of heaven entirely so that he could no longer accuse the people of God before the Father. Therefore it is Michael rather than Christ who expelled Satan from heaven.

2. Reread **Revelation 12:10–12.** What is the basis of our confidence and joy before the throne of God?

3. What is the word of warning in this hymn for people still on earth?

4. In what ways does Paul in **Romans 8:1, 31–39** offer assurance similar to that found in **Revelation 12:10–12?**

War on Earth

Although through His victory on the cross Christ conquered Satan and eliminated his right to stand before God to accuse and condemn the people of God, this is not yet the end of the matter. Satan is on earth and earnestly seeks to persecute "the woman who had given birth to the male child," that is, the church **(Revelation 12:13).** As we learned in **Revelation 12:6,** God carries away the woman into the desert, the place of refuge. Here the church is sustained in the midst of opposition and difficulties for "a time, times and half a time," the period from the cross to the Last Day.

1. What significance do you see in the similarity between **Revelation 12:14** and **Exodus 19:3–6,** which uses similar phraseology?

2. According to **Revelation 12:17,** on whom does Satan make war?

3. According to **Revelation 12:11,** through what do God's people overcome Satan?

4. According to **Revelation 12** what kind of experiences can you expect as a Christian in this world? What joy and confidence do you find in this chapter?

For Next Time
Read **Revelation 13:1–14:20.**

Now have come the salvation and the power and the kingdom of our God, and the authority of His Christ. Revelation 12:10

Lesson 8

The War Intensifies

Bible Basis
Revelation 13:1–14:20

The Beast from the Sea

Read **Revelation 13:1–10.** Here John describes his vision of a beast that arises from the sea to assist Satan in his warfare against God and humanity, in particular the church (the woman and her offspring).

The sea with all its turbulence and violent power is an apt figure to depict the agitated condition of sinful humankind and the seething cauldron of national and social life. Out of this sea come those political, economic, and social powers that presume to take the place of God and seek to wield absolute authority over the lives and souls of people.

As the beast emerges, John sees the hideous "ten horns and seven heads, with ten crowns on his horns" **(v. 1).** Perhaps the seven heads stress the beast's relationship to the seven-headed dragon of **chapter 12** from whom this beast receives its power and authority. First-century readers might possibly have seen in this a reference to Rome with its seven hills.

The 10 horns likely represent all anti-Christian governments that will arise and put themselves in the place of God. (Recall that horns symbolize strength and political power.) The 10 crowns on the horns rather than on the heads suggest that these governments gain their position and power by the use of brute force. Here as in the description of the dragon in **Revelation 12:3** the Greek word for crown—*diadēma*—refers to the type worn by Persian kings and indicates that the wearer claims to be God. Note also the blasphemous names written on each head of the beast.

As the beast continues to emerge, John sees its body which looks like leopard, large and fierce, ready to pounce upon its prey. As the beast steps out of the water, John sees that its feet are those of a bear ready to rend and tear. The mouth is that of a lion eager to devour all of God's good creation.

In this chapter we meet an unholy trinity, whose beings are antithetical to the three persons of the Godhead. God the Father gave Jesus all authority in heaven and on earth **(Matthew 28:18)**. Here Satan gives the beast "his power and his throne and great authority" **(Revelation 13:2)**. And both the dragon and the beast receive the worship of people.

But the dragon and the beast—as powerful as they are—have only the authority allowed them by God. God permits the beast to exercise its authority for 42 months, the period of this Gospel age from the time of Christ to the Last Day **(13:5)**.

The fatal wound that has been healed **(13:3)** may be a parody of the wounds of Christ. Jesus died and rose again and still bears the marks of His crucifixion. This beast bears a wound that appears to have been fatal but was not.

This wound also suggests that when one tyrannical power has been subdued, another arises to take its place. So the world will continue to have a series of tyrannical powers until the Lord returns on the Last Day.

1. The ancient seer Daniel had a vision similar to that of John. Compare **Daniel 7:1–28** with **Revelation 13:1–10**. Identify at least three similarities between these two visions.

2. Images used by John in **Revelation 13** appear in other parts of the Bible. Identify those images as they appear in the texts below.
  a. **Revelation 13:1/Isaiah 17:12**

  b. **Revelation 13:2/Daniel 7:6; Hosea 13:7; Habakkuk 1:5–8**

  c. **Revelation 13:2/Proverbs 17:12; Hosea 13:8**

d. **Revelation 13:2/Psalm 17:12; Hosea 5:14–15; 13:7; 1 Peter 5:8**

3. What does **Revelation 13:7** say the beast was given power to do?

4. Throughout biblical history tyrannical powers persecuted and suppressed the people of God. Name three such powers and describe how they persecuted God's people. Which power did John have in mind as he wrote **Revelation**?

5. Name at least one great power in recent times that arose to oppress the people of God. What were some tactics used to suppress Christians?

6. In your opinion, does Satan ever use the government of your country today to suppress Christians? If so, in what ways?

7. Although it is Satan who uses civil government to tyrannize and suppress God's people, God overrules these evil designs and uses them to accomplish His own purposes. According to **Hosea 5:14–15** and **13:9–11,** what is one such purpose?

8. Read **Acts 5:29; Romans 13:1–7; 1 Timothy 2:1–6; Titus 3:1–2;** and **1 Peter 2:11–17.** How does the institution of government itself fit into God's care for our sinful world? What is to be your attitude as a Christian

toward your government? Is civil disobedience ever justified? Explain your answer.

9. What does it mean to "worship the beast" **(Revelation 13:4, 8)?**

10. Who worships the beast and who does not **(v. 8)?**

11. A natural response of sinners is to meet force with force. What does **Revelation 13:9–10** suggest about the desirability (or effectiveness) of the church using force to protect itself or achieve its goals (see also **Matthew 26:50–54**)? What is your opinion about the church encouraging civil government to pass and enforce laws to help the church achieve its goals? If the church is not to use force, what means does it have to fulfill its mission and to protect itself from its enemies (see **Ephesians 6:10–20**)?

The Beast out of the Earth

Read **Revelation 13:11–18,** which describes a second beast. In contrast to the first beast that arises from the sea and has a ferocious appearance, the second beast arises from the more familiar land and is less fearsome in appearance.

1. What might be the significance of the fact that this beast has two horns like a lamb (see **Revelation 5:6**)?

2. What characteristic of the beast reveals its true character?

3. Many scholars think that this beast symbolizes false teachers and their human philosophies. What does Jesus warn about false prophets in **Matthew 7:15–20?**

4. Note that the second beast exercises authority on behalf of the first beast to the end that the people of the world will worship the first beast **(Revelation 13:12).** In this capacity to which person of the Trinity is the second beast antithetical?

5. How does the second beast deceive? Compare this with Jesus' statement in **Matthew 24:23–24.**

6. Whom does this beast deceive?

7. What are the consequences for those who refuse to worship the image of the first beast or to receive the mark of the beast?

Although this section does not specifically say to which beast the mark belongs, the relationship of the two beasts would indicate that it belongs to the first beast. This is confirmed later in **Revelation (19:19–20).** Those who receive the beast's mark do so in a prominent place. The mark symbolizes allegiance to the beast and may be a parody of the seal placed on the foreheads of the servants of God in **Revelation 7:3–4.**

There have been numerous attempts to identify the symbolism of the number 666, but it is perhaps best to see it as the number of the unholy trinity, each digit of which falls short of the complete number *seven.* Although the unholy trinity of Satan, worldly tyranny, and false religion claim the place of God, their claim falls short, and they will not prevail in the end.

The Triumph of the Saints

Read **Revelation 14:1–5.** John was given a vision of the saints in heaven to encourage him and all Christians to persevere in faith by the power of the Spirit in spite of the allurements, temptations, and persecutions in the world. Here we see the Lamb (Jesus) standing on the heavenly Mount Zion.

1. Who are the 144,000 who are with Jesus?

2. Instead of the mark of the beast, what do these people have on their foreheads?

In great joy because of the victory won and in thanksgiving to the Lamb who delivered them, the saints of God join in a new song—new because their residence in heaven with its eternal bliss and peace is a new experience. This song is at once majestic and sublime ("like the roar of rushing waters and like a loud peal of thunder," **v. 2**) and also lovely, sweet, and tender ("like that of harpists playing their harps," **v. 2**). This song reflects the experience of having been purchased by the precious blood of the Lamb; therefore only the saints, those who share in this experience, can learn this song.

3. Recalling that idolatry is often pictured as unfaithfulness to God, what does it mean that these saints are virgins (see **2 Corinthians 11:2**)?

Rather than following Satan and his beasts, these saints follow the Lamb. They were purchased by Christ and offered as firstfruits—a choice offering—to Himself and the Father. Because of the redeeming, cleansing blood of Christ, these saints now stand blameless before the eternal throne.

The Mission of the Angels

Read **Revelation 14:6–13.** In His grace and mercy God continues to delay His coming in order that all people might repent of their rebellion against Him and be led to faith in Jesus Christ by the Spirit's operation through the Gospel. In this section John in a vision sees the sending of the angels just prior to the Last Day to warn all people of impending judgment.

The mission of the first angel **(14:6–7)** is especially to those who in their absorption with the challenges and charms of this world are unconcerned and indifferent about their future and eternal well-being. The mission of the first angel, through God's people on earth, is to call on all humankind to fear God and prepare for the impending hour of judgment.

Through the proclamation of the Law and Gospel, God's people throughout the ages until the end of this age are to call people to repentance and to place their trust for salvation in Jesus Christ alone. The second and third angels warn against placing one's ultimate trust in the things and powers of this age, which are tools Satan uses to mislead humankind away from God and eternal life.

Babylon symbolizes all the enemies of God's people. Like the two beasts of **chapter 13,** Babylon has led the nations into adultery against God. Here the angel announces that this great enemy has fallen.

The warning of the third angel **(14:9–12)** seems to be directed to those who place their ultimate trust in the political powers of this world. At the Last Day all human institutions will come to an end. Then it will be obvious for all to see that all ultimate power and good resides in God alone—the God who has revealed Himself in His Son Jesus Christ.

More than that, having in their lifetime spurned the grace of God in Jesus Christ, these people will now be given justice. The angel in **14:10–11** describes what we truly deserve from God because of our rebellion against Him. If we ignore or reject God's offer of grace mediated by the first angel through the church, this is our just reward.

But those who by the Spirit receive and persevere in the grace of God in Jesus Christ in spite of all earthly obstacles and temptations can anticipate an eternity of blessedness **(14:12–13).**

1. According to Jesus in **Luke 17:26–30,** what is a major cause for peo-

ple inheriting eternal destruction?

2. Give three examples showing how people in our day demonstrate their indifference to warnings of judgment and to the Gospel. What evidences of complacency, if any, do you detect in Christianity today? How would you overcome this kind of spirit?

3. What are some opportunities that you personally have for being involved in the mission and message of the first angel?

4. Why is it difficult to endure patiently, obey God's commandments, and remain faithful to Jesus (14:12)? Do you think it is more difficult today to persevere than in former ages? Explain your opinion.

The Final Harvest

Read **Revelation 14:14–20.** As with other cycles of John's visions, this one ends with the Day of Judgment.

1. How does **Matthew 13:24–30** help you understand this passage?

2. What does the description of the Son of Man in **Daniel 7:13–14** suggest about the Son of Man in **Revelation 14:14?**

3. What reassurances for your personal life did you receive from your study of **Revelation 13–14?**

For Next Time
Read **Revelation 15:1–16:21.**

Blessed are the dead who die in the Lord. Revelation 14:13

Lesson 9

The Third Cycle of Tribulations: The Seven Bowls

Bible Basis
Revelation 15:1–16:21

Introduction

Like a crescendo, the events depicted in each cycle in **Revelation** move toward the grand climax of Judgment Day. In the first cycle of earthly events leading to the Last Day **(Revelation 6:1–8:5)**, the visions emphasize the evils and tribulations caused by human sin and focus on the church's being sealed by God in spite of all persecution.

The second cycle **(Revelation 8:6–11:19)** stresses evils in nature, as well as the effect of the devil's forces, that cause people to suffer. Yet in the midst of persecution the church witnesses triumphantly to the Lamb who was slain for the salvation of all humankind.

Now in the third earthly cycle, the visions reveal the final judgments of God poured out on humankind. The church in the meantime sings and celebrates God's judgment on the devil's evil forces and thus the ultimate triumph of the Gospel.

The Church Triumphant

John is now going to tell us about the outpouring of God's wrath on all those who steadfastly resist repenting of their sin and turning to the Savior God gives us all. But before He describes the outpouring of the bowls of God's wrath on unrepentant humankind, he describes the glorious state of the faithful saints in heaven.

Read **Revelation 15:1–8.**

1. What previous sign is implied with "another great and marvelous sign" in **15:1** (see **12:1–3**)?

2. What parallel is there between **Revelation 15:1–2** and **Exodus 14:21–31?**

3. Who are those who are "victorious over the beast and his image and over the number of his name" **(v. 2)?**

4. What similarity do you see between **Revelation 15:2–4** and **Exodus 15:1–18?**

5. What is the "tabernacle of the Testimony" **(v. 5; Exodus 25:8–9; 40:34–35)?** What does this figure indicate about the source of the outpourings of the bowls about to follow?

6. What does the smoke indicate **(v. 8)?** See **Exodus 40:34–35; 1 Kings 8:1, 10–11; Isaiah 6:1–8;** and **Ezekiel 44:4.**

7. What does the gold used for the bowls symbolize **(15:7)?** What significance is there in that the bowls were filled with the wrath of God? What

does the ascription of eternity to God in this verse suggest about the finality and duration of divine judgment on unrepentant humankind?

Plagues of Nature

Read **Revelation 16:1–9.** Here we see a strong resemblance to the plagues of Egypt that preceded the exodus (recorded in **Exodus 7:14–11:10**) as well as to the first four plagues in the trumpet cycle **(8:6–12).**

1. What is affected by the first four plagues?

2. What similarity do you find between **Revelation 16:1–9** and **Matthew 24:29–31?**

3. Who suffers from the first plague?

4. Why is the third plague a just punishment for God's enemies?

5. What does **Revelation 16:9** imply about one of the purposes for these plagues?

6. What encouragement, if any, is there in this vision for you to persevere in the faith and to be diligent in witnessing to our Lord and Savior Jesus Christ?

Plagues among the Nations

Read **Revelation 16:10–16.**

History suggests that there is an ebb and flow in the age-old conflict between the forces of God and those of Satan. But now in John's revelation God's patience finally is exhausted, and the angels continue to pour out the bowls of God's wrath. This judgment will occur not only through phenomena in nature, but also in the political sphere.

Just before the Last Day, darkness will cover the kingdom of the beast. This is the beast from the sea introduced in **Revelation 13.** Great anti-Christian powers in which people placed their trust will collapse totally. This will cause these people enormous suffering, but they will still refuse to repent.

The Euphrates River, subject of the sixth bowl judgment, is an allusion to all great powers that oppress and destroy the people of God. Assyria and Babylon—some of Israel's worst oppressors in the Old Testament—were located in the region of the Euphrates. The drying of the waters symbolizes the removal of a barrier that prevents God's enemies from giving full vent to their oppression.

John sees three evil spirits coming from the mouth of the dragon (Satan), the mouth of the beast (the beast from the sea, representing anti-Christian political power), and the mouth of the false prophet (called the beast from the earth in **Revelation 13**). These demonic spirits perform miraculous signs and gather the leaders of the world for one last battle against God at a place called Armageddon.

Armageddon quite possibly is a reference to the region around Megiddo, a city near Mt. Carmel, where the Israelites overcame their enemies under Deborah **(Judges 4:1–5:31)** and where Elijah confronted the prophets of Baal **(1 Kings 18:16–40).** A literal, geographic place is not meant here; Armageddon is a symbol for the final overthrow of evil by God.

In this vision there is no more reference to this force gathered for battle. Perhaps God upstages the battle by bringing the world to an end before it begins. The same sequence will be shown to John again in coming visions.

"Behold, I come like a thief! Blessed is he who stays awake and keeps his clothes with him" **(16:15).** This statement by Jesus is similar to statements made by Him in the gospels concerning His second coming (see **Matthew 24:42–44**). Not only are God's people to be prepared for these last evil days, but they also are to recognize in these catastrophic events the final coming of the Lord.

The End of All Things

Read **Revelation 16:17–21.** As with the seventh seal and the seventh trumpet, the seventh bowl is the end. God's mercy has been exhausted, and He brings this age to a definite conclusion.

1. Note the similarities between the visions of the last trumpet and the final bowl.

a. **Revelation 11:15** and **16:17**

b. **Revelation 11:19** and **16:18, 21**

2. What does "the cup filled with the wine of the fury of [God's] wrath" **(Revelation 11:19)** symbolize (see **Isaiah 51:17; Jeremiah 25:15–16; Habakkuk 2:16**)? Who must drink it? Who drank it for us (see **Matthew 26:36–46**)?

3. What does **Revelation 16:21** indicate about the apparent hardness of heart toward God and His Son that many people bear?

4. Compare **Revelation 16:9** with **16:21.** Why is repentance mentioned in the first passage, but not in the second?

5. Contrast the curses of the unbelievers in **Revelation 16:9, 21** with the praise of the saints in **Revelation 15:3.**

6. What message of hope for yourself do you find in this section?

For Next Time
Read **Revelation 17:1–18:24.**

Great and marvelous are Your deeds, Lord God Almighty. Just and true are Your ways, King of the ages. Who will not fear You, O Lord, and bring glory to Your name? For You alone are holy. All nations will come and worship before You, for Your righteous acts have been revealed. Revelation 15:3–4

Lesson 10

The Fall of Babylon

Bible Basis
Revelation 17:1–18:24

Introduction

Twice before in his visions John has been assured of the destruction of Babylon the Great **(Revelation 14:8; 16:19).** This section concentrates on that destruction

The Prostitute and the Beast

Read **Revelation 17:1–18.**

An angel having one of the seven bowls tells John that he will be shown "the punishment of the great prostitute, who sits on many waters" **(Revelation 17:1).** The reference to many waters is an allusion to the city of Babylon, which sat on the banks of the Euphrates and had many canals. (Babylon is described this way in **Jeremiah 51:13.**) But before John actually sees her punishment, he is shown more about her and about the beast on which she sits.

1. Why is Babylon called a prostitute?

2. What is meant by adultery (see **Jeremiah 3:6–10; Ezekiel 16:20–32**)?

3. Who commits adultery with the prostitute **(Revelation 17:2)**?

Babylon

The historical city of Babylon was located on the banks of the Euphrates River. This city was the center of a great empire that around 600 B.C. ruled most of the ancient Near East from the Persian Gulf to the Mediterranean Sea. Babylon was used by God to discipline His people for their unfaithfulness to Him. In 605 B.C. and 597 B.C. Babylon invaded Judah and carried some of its residents back to the area around Babylon. Finally in 586 B.C., Nebuchadnezzar, the great Babylonian king, destroyed the city of Jerusalem, including the temple of God and carried even more exiles into captivity. These people were deported to a pagan land where they were always tempted to participate in pagan worship and sometimes were threatened with force if they did not do so (see **Daniel 3**). The terror and the shame of the Babylonian Exile made it a powerful image in the minds of God's people for centuries to follow. It is easy to see why Babylon is a powerful symbol of the enemies of God's people.

In the years before the exile, God sent prophets to warn His people of their impending doom and to call them to repentance. Even as God's prophets were prophesying that Judah would be taken captive by Babylon, they were also prophesying the destruction of Babylon **(Isaiah 21:9; Jeremiah 50–51)**. Babylon was crushed by Cyrus the Persian in 539 B.C. Cyrus then encouraged the people of Judah to return to their land and rebuild their temple.

Just as the faithful people of God in the Old Testament looked forward to and rejoiced in the coming destruction of Babylon, so God's faithful people in the New Testament era can look forward to and rejoice in the ultimate destruction of all of God's enemies.

There have been numerous attempts to specifically identify the "Babylon" of which John wrote. Certainly in John's day, the powerful, arrogant, pagan Roman Empire, which set itself in the place of God and at times persecuted God's people, was an embodiment of Babylon. But in every age God's people face such enemies.

---

4. What is the condition of the inhabitants of the earth (unbelievers)? What does this condition symbolize?

5. What makes this prostitute so alluring **(17:4; 18:3, 9–19)**?

6. In her hand the prostitute holds a golden cup from which she offers her lovers the wine that intoxicates them. What is the true nature of what this cup holds **(17:4)?**

7. What does the prostitute's title reveal about her **(17:5)?**

8. What is symbolized in **17:6** (see also **18:24**)?

9. What is the extent of this woman's influence **(17:15; 18:23)?**

10. Compare **Revelation 17:3, 8–12** with **Revelation 13:1–4.** What does the beast on which the prostitute rides symbolize?

11. What is the reaction of the inhabitants of the earth to this beast?

12. What causes their reaction (**17:8; 13:3**)? What does this symbolize?

13. Compare **Revelation 17:8** with **Revelation 4:8.** What does this indicate about the beast? From where does the beast come?

Interpreting the Prostitute, the Beast, and the Kings

The prostitute sits on the beast. She is supported by the beast (for a time) and works in conjunction with the beast. There is obviously a political aspect to the prostitute herself (see **17:18**), so it is difficult to clearly separate her role from that of the beast. But that is not of concern here. What is important is to see that political forces that put themselves in the place of God aid and abet the luring of people into idolatry.

The imagery of this chapter is rather fluid in places. In **17:9** the seven heads represent seven hills, an obvious reference to Rome which was built on seven hills. The seven heads also represent seven kings (**17:10**).

One likely interpretation of **17:10** is as follows: The five kings who have fallen represent the Old Testament empires who at one time or another threatened the people of God with annihilation: Egypt prior to the exodus; Assyria which destroyed the kingdom of Israel; Babylon which took the kingdom of Judah into captivity; Persia under Xerxes, who ordered the killing of the people of Judah; and the empire of Alexander the Great that spawned the cruel Antiochus Epiphanes. The sixth king represents the Roman Empire. The seventh had not yet come at the time of John.

---

14. The beast himself, who had previously been symbolic of all anti-Christian kingdoms, symbolizes an eighth king. What will be the fate of that king?

15. The 10 kings of **17:12** likely represent the complete number of anti-Christian governments (recall that 10 is the number of completeness). Their reign is short ("one hour") and their authority limited. What is the one purpose of these kings and the beast to whom they give their authority **(17:13–14)?**

16. Jesus, the Lamb of God our Savior who lived died and rose again for us, will win the ultimate victory over all evil. Why will the Lamb be victorious? Who accompanies Him in victory?

17. At whose hand does Babylon the Great meet her destruction **(17:16)?** Who is working behind the scenes?

Babylon Has Fallen!

Read **Revelation 18:1–24.**

John hears the prophetic announcement that Babylon has fallen. Yet he and his readers know that although it will surely happen, it is still to come.

1. What warning is given the people of God in **18:4** (see also **2 Corinthians 6:14–18**).

2. When the hour of Babylon's destruction comes, how quickly will she fall **(18:8, 10)?**

3. Why will those who have fallen under her spell **(18:23)** mourn her death **(18:9–19)**?

4. What is the extent of her fall **(18:6–8, 21–23)**?

5. What should be the reaction of the people of God to Babylon's fall **(18:20, 24)**? Why?

For Next Time
Read **Revelation 19:1–21.**

Rejoice over her, O heaven! Rejoice, saints and apostles and prophets! God has judged her for the way she treated you. Revelation 18:20

Lesson 11

The Victory Is Won

Bible Basis
Revelation 19:1–21

The Victory Song

Recall the great victory for God's people that John saw in **Revelation 18.** Following that victory, John heard a joyous celebration in heaven. Read about that celebration in **Revelation 19:1–4.**

Hallelujah means "praise the Lord." According to these verses, why do God's people praise the Lord?

Marriage Feast of the Lamb

Read **Revelation 19:5–10.** To better understand this section, it is helpful to know something about ancient Jewish marriage customs. First there was the betrothal (somewhat similar to our engagement but much more binding) performed before witnesses. In this ceremony God's blessing was pronounced on the pair and from that day forward they were regarded as husband and wife (see **2 Corinthians 11:2** where Paul "betrothed" Christians to Christ).

During the interval between the betrothal and the wedding feast, the groom paid the dowry to the bride's father. At the end of this interval there was a procession for which the bride had prepared and adorned herself. Clothed in his best attire and accompanied by his friends (who bore torches and sang), the groom proceeded to the home of his betrothed to receive her and bring her to his own home or that of his parents. Finally, there was the wedding feast which often lasted 7 or even 14 days.

W. Hendriksen (*More Than Conquerors*, p. 216) describes this celestial wedding thus: In Christ the bride was *chosen* already in eternity. Throughout the Old Testament period *the wedding was announced.* When the Son of God assumed human flesh for our salvation, *the betrothal took place.* Christ *paid the dowry price* with His substitutionary life, suffering, and death for the salvation of all humankind. After an *interval* (the entire period from Christ's ascension to the Last Day), Christ will return to receive and accompany His bride, the church, to the heavenly *wedding feast.*

1. How in the following passages is the relationship between the Lord and His people compared to that of a bridegroom and his bride?

a. **Isaiah 62:5**

b. **Jeremiah 2:31–32**

c. **2 Corinthians 11:2**

d. **Ephesians 5:25–32**

e. **Revelation 21:9–10**

2. The New Evangelical Translation translates the latter part of **19:8** in this way: "For the fine linen consists of the verdicts of 'not guilty' pronounced on the believers." Compare this translation with **Revelation 7:3–4** and **Isaiah 61:10.**

3. What is the significance of the phrase that this "fine linen, bright and clean, was *given* her to wear" **(19:8)?**

4. What important truth about angels is given in **19:10?**

The Victor Receives His Victory

Read **Revelation 19:11–21.** This section describes the second coming of Jesus to judge the world in righteousness and to destroy His enemies.

1. Who is the rider on the white horse **(19:11)?** What does the description "Faithful and True" indicate about the character of the rider and whether we can depend on Him? What does the color of the horse symbolize?

2. According to **Revelation 19:11–12,** what has the rider appeared to do?

3. What is the significance of eyes "like blazing fire" (**19:12** see also **Revelation 1:14; 2:18**)?

4. The Greek word for crown in **Revelation 19:12** is *diadēma*, the kind worn by Persian kings indicating that the wearer claims to be God. Here the crowns (many of them) are worn by Him who has the right to wear them. What might be the blood in which the rider's robe is dipped (**19:13**; see also **Isaiah 63:1–6**)?

5. According to **John 1:1, 14; 14:8–10,** what does it mean that Jesus is the "Word of God"?

6. What is the sword with which the rider strikes down the nations (**19:15;** see also **Isaiah 49:2; Hebrews 4:12; Ephesians 6:17**)?

7. What do the quotation from **Psalm 2:9** in **Revelation 19:15** and the name of the rider in **19:16** indicate about Him?

8. What does **19:18** indicate about who will be defeated?

The Enemy's Final Defeat

In **Revelation 19:19–21** John is again shown the great army gathered for battle that he saw in **Revelation 16:12–21.** Here he is shown a different aspect of the same scene—this one focuses on the complete and final destruction of the beast from the sea and the beast from the earth (here called the false prophet). This great army is arrayed to fight against the rider on the white horse and his army. But as in **chapter 16,** the battle is not described. Perhaps none took place.

What John sees is the victory of the King of kings and the Lord of lords over all earthly kingdoms opposed to Him (the beast from sea) and over all philosophies and religions that would lead people away from Christ in whom alone is salvation (the beast from the earth).

This evidently is the fulfillment of Ezekiel's prophecy concerning the defeat of Gog and his armies. See **Ezekiel 38–39,** especially **vv. 17–24** and **Revelation 20:7–10.**

Revelation 19:21 is especially meaningful. It reminds us that it is the Word of God that judges people. For those who reject Christ and His salvation, the Word of God is the instrument of judgment and eternal destruction, while for those whom the Spirit brings to faith through the Gospel it is the means of life.

9. What encouragements did you find in **Revelation 19** to remain steadfast, by the power of the Spirit, in your relationship with Christ?

For Next Time

Read **Revelation 20:1–15.**

Then the angel said to me, "Write: 'Blessed are those who are invited to the wedding supper of the Lamb!' " And he added, "These are the true words of God." Revelation 19:9

Lesson 12

The Millennium

Bible Basis
Revelation 20:1–15

Introduction

Because of the attention given by many people in the recent past to millennialism, **Revelation 20** is of particular interest. Theories of millennialism are based on this chapter, so it will be useful to closely examine it.

The Millennium

Before examining the various theories of millennialism, it probably is best to review the classical interpretation of the chapter. Then we will be in a better position to evaluate the theories.

In **Revelation 20** we have the second grand sweeping view of history from the time of the earthly ministry of Jesus until the Last Day. In several previous scenes, we were shown the defeat of some of God's enemies. In **chapters 17–18** we saw the destruction of Babylon. **Chapter 19** revealed the end of the two beasts. Now in **Revelation 20** the end of Satan and death are described.

Read **Revelation 20:1–10. Verses 1–9** provide the background for the judgment on Satan in **verse 10.** John sees an angel descend from heaven to bind Satan in the abyss (hell) for 1,000 years (the symbolic number for a complete period of time). The purpose is to prevent Satan from deceiving the nations until the end of this period of time. While Satan is bound, he still is able to influence and tempt human beings. But he does not have free course to deceive the nations and gather them for a final assault against God and His people **(Revelation 20:8).**

The binding of Satan occurred with the saving life, death, resurrection, and ascension of Christ (see **Mark 3:22–27; Revelation 12:5–12; Luke 10:17–18**). Prior to that time the nations were under the dominion of Satan. Pagan worship abounded everywhere. Only one nation, the relatively insignificant Hebrew people, had been chosen by God to bear witness to His promises of salvation. Yet even this people was more often unfaithful to God than not. **Acts 14:16** describes that historical situation.

But during the long period during which Satan was loose and the nations generally followed false gods, the Lord encouraged His people with the assurance that when the Messiah came, He would conquer Satan and inaugurate an age in which people from many nations would come to a saving relationship with the only true God.

1. What promise is contained in each of the following passages?

   a. **Genesis 12:3**

   b. **Psalm 2:8**

   c. **Psalm 72:8–11**

   d. **Isaiah 42:6**

   e. **Isaiah 60:1–3**

   f. **Amos 9:11–12**

g. **Micah 4:1–2**

2. The binding of Satan began with the coming of Jesus of Nazareth into the world and was completed with His death and resurrection. Many passages from the gospels describe the conflict between Jesus and Satan during Jesus' earthly ministry. Only a few are listed below. What aspect of the binding of Satan do you find in each of them?
   a. **Matthew 4:1–11; Luke 4:1–13**

b. **Mark 1:34; 3:20–30**

c. **Mark 5:1–20**

d. **Mark 1:21–28**

e. **John 12:30–33**

A Thousand Years

The entire New Testament period is the "thousand years" (the period of completeness) during which Satan is bound and the proclamation of the Gospel has free course **(20:1–3).**

This Gospel of forgiveness frees people from the power of Satan. **Matthew 16:17–20; 18:15–18;** and **John 20:21–23** speak of the ministry given by Jesus to the church of forgiving the sins of penitent sinners and thus saving them from slavery to Satan.

Revelation 20:4–6 describes the period of the Gospel age from the perspective of heaven. The *souls* of all those who were put to death because of their faith (a reference to all who die in faith) reign with Christ in heaven from the time of their temporal death to the resurrection at the Last Day. (The New Evangelical Translation translates the last line of **verse 4** as follows: "and they lived and ruled with Christ for a thousand years.")

The dead who rejected Christ in this life do not share in this heavenly life with Him during the thousand years **(20:5).** What happens to them after the thousand years is discussed in **verses 11–15.**

3. The living and reigning with Christ on the part of the saints is called the first resurrection. Some maintain that since the conversion of the sinner is referred to in Scripture as a resurrection, the first resurrection can be thought of as starting with one's conversion (see **Romans 6:1–11; Ephesians 2:4–6; Colossians 3:1**). What is the second resurrection **(Isaiah 26:19; Daniel 12:2–3; Matthew 24:31; 1 Corinthians 15:42–57; 1 Thessalonians 4:13–18)?**

4. What is the second death **(Revelation 2:11; 19:20; 20:6, 14; 21:8; Matthew 25:41, 46; 2 Thessalonians 1:8–9)?**

Satan's Doom

Reread **Revelation 20:7–10.** The day of opportunity for the church's worldwide mission endeavors will not last forever. Toward the close of the New Testament era (the thousand years) and just before the Last Day, God will, for a short time **(20:3)**, permit Satan to make one final, all-out attack against the followers of God.

Satan will go out to deceive the nations; from throughout the world he will gather a force of people who despise the Word of God and reject God's gracious offer of life and salvation through Jesus Christ alone. (For Jesus' description of these days just before the end see **Matthew 24:15–31; Luke 21:10–28**). This great uprising of nations will be the last protest against the church. (In Jewish apocalyptic literature, Gog and Magog, which are mentioned in the Old Testament, became symbols for all the forces of evil.)

As we saw in **Revelation 16:12–21** and **19:19–21** (where this force gathered for battle is also pictured), no attention is given to the battle itself if it even occurs. Here fire comes down from heaven and devours the force. Satan, the last great enemy of God and His people, is cast into the fire of hell entirely separated from God and His goodness.

The Great Judgment

Read **Revelation 20:11–15**. After John sees Satan's final defeat, he is shown another picture of the Last Day. On that day the earth will be completely destroyed and all humankind from every period of history will be raised and judged by Christ. The criterion is "according to what they had done" **(20:12)**. According to this standard, all people will be condemned to eternal death in hell. However, there will be some whose names have been written in the book of life **(20:12)**. These are the people who acknowledged their inability to do God's will and who placed their trust solely in the saving merits, life, and work of Christ. They will be spared the second death and will live with God in eternal bliss **(Revelation 21–22)**.

What great comfort is found in **Revelation 20:14?**

Millennial Theories

The view of millennialism just described is sometimes called *amillennialism*. Two theories at variance with this scriptural view are known as premillennialism and postmillennialism.

Premillennialism is a general term for a variety of views that seem to have in common belief in the following events.

   a. Before the great tribulation, Christ will return invisibly to remove all believers from the world so that they need not suffer these troubles. The raising and transfiguration of the saints is understood as the *rapture* supposedly described in **1 Thessalonians 4:16–17.**

   b. There will be a great tribulation of seven years in the midst of which the Antichrist will be revealed. God's wrath will be poured upon the nations so fully that the nation of Israel will accept Christ as Savior.

c. Once Israel has accepted Him, Christ will establish His millennial kingdom. In this first judgment He will judge all nations according to their treatment of the Jews. During this millennium all messianic promises will be literally fulfilled. Toward the end of this period Satan will be loosed for a time to make a final assault against Christ and will be destroyed.

d. At the end of the millennium the second resurrection will occur. After the judgment at the great white throne, death and hell will be destroyed and God will create a new heaven and a new earth to endure forever.

Dispensationalism is quite similar to premillennialism except it envisions seven eras of dispensations: (a) the age of Eden up to Adam's fall; (b) the age of the rule of conscience which extended from the expulsion from paradise to the flood; (c) the era of human government introduced with the establishment of capital punishment **(Genesis 9:6)** to the destruction of Sodom; (d) the era of the patriarchs that ended with the destruction of Pharaoh's army at the Red Sea; (e) the Mosaic period beginning with Sinai and ending with Christ's crucifixion; (f) the Christian era that began with Pentecost and that will end with the great tribulation, the judgment of the nations, and the destruction of the Antichrist; and (g) the era of manifestation ushered in by the rapture and the glorious manifestation of Jesus to His followers; this era will end with the destruction of Satan and the judgment on the great white throne to be followed by eternal life for believers and eternal condemnation for unbelievers.

Postmillennialism differs in that it holds that Christ's second coming will occur *after* the millennium rather than *before*. It holds that this world is gradually being Christianized, which will result in a long period of peace and prosperity called the millennium. This period will conclude with the Second Coming of Christ, the resurrection of the dead, the final judgment, and the eternal destiny of humankind in either heaven or hell.

Of course, millennialism has many variations and nuances of thought that are impossible to describe briefly.

Over against these varied views of the millennium we have clear passages of Scripture that enable us to anticipate the Second Coming of Christ with clarity of thought and confidence of heart.

1. Why can we anticipate Jesus' Second Coming and Judgment Day with joy and confidence in spite of our sin and unworthiness **(Romans 5:9; Galatians 4:4–5; 2 Timothy 1:10; Hebrews 2:14)**?

2. For what purposes has God placed us in this world (**Genesis 1:28–29; 2:15; Acts 1:6–8; Ephesians 5:1–21; 1 Timothy 2:1–4; 1 Peter 2:9**)?

3. What happens to us at the end of our earthly life (**Philippians 1:21–26**)?

4. When will Christ's Second Coming really occur? What will happen to us, His followers, on that day (**John 6:40; 1 Corinthians 15:35–57; 1 Thessalonians 4:13–18**)?

5. Why is it futile to try to predict the time when Christ will return again (**Matthew 24:36, 42**)?

6. Can we anticipate an era of general peace and prosperity in this world prior to Christ's Second Coming? Why or why not (**Matthew 24:3–14; 2 Peter 3:3–10**)? To what do these optimistic passages refer (**Isaiah 2:2–4; 11:6–9; Joel 2:23–32; Zechariah 9:9–10**)?

7. Only one New Testament passage (**1 Thessalonians 4:13–17**) speaks clearly of the rapture. What is the rapture of which this passage speaks?

8. Why can't we state that either all Jews or all Gentiles eventually will be saved (**Romans 9:6–8; 11:25–26**)?

This chapter is a source of great encouragement when we suffer in one way or another because of our faith. Instead of engaging in idle speculation, one does better to meditate upon its message and derive the comfort and hope to be found there.

For Next Time

Read **Revelation 21:1–22:21.**

And I saw the dead, great and small, standing before the throne, and books were opened. Another book was opened, which is the book of life. Revelation 20:12

Lesson 13

The New Jerusalem

Bible Basis
Revelation 21:1–22:21

Introduction

If you had your druthers, what kind of world would you want this to be? People as diverse as Plato (*The Republic*), Thomas More (*Utopia*), and B. F. Skinner (*Walden Two*) have described what they considered to be the ideal society and how it might be attained. You too probably have your view of what a perfect world would be like.

We have a unique description of a perfect world in the last two chapters of **Revelation**—unique in that this description is based on reality. Here we have a picture of what the world will eventually be like for the people of God—a vision that still lies in the future but which can be partially realized already in this life.

In some interesting ways the last two chapters of the Bible and the first three chapters of the Bible parallel and contrast with each other. Note the parallel or contrast in each set of passages below.

1. **Genesis 1:1/Revelation 21:1**

2. **Genesis 1:14–19/Revelation 21:23–25; 22:5**

3. **Genesis 3:1/Revelation 21:8**

4. Genesis 3:8/Revelation 21:3

5. Genesis 3:16–19/Revelation 22:3

6. Genesis 3:22/Revelation 22:14

7. Genesis 3:22–24/Revelation 22:2

As we study this section, as well as other parts of **Revelation,** we must remember that John wrote of matters beyond our experiences in this world. To enable us to understand the message, the Holy Spirit through John used figures of speech that draw on our earthly concepts and experiences. Therefore we need to keep in mind that here we have a spiritual, not a literal, description of the new heaven and the new earth.

A New Heaven and a New Earth

Read **Revelation 21:1–8.**

1. What does **Revelation 21:1** say about the permanence of this present universe (see also **Isaiah 34:4, 12; Matthew 24:32–35; 2 Peter 3:10; Revelation 6:14; 20:11–15**)?

2. What relationship do you see between **Revelation 21:1** and **Isaiah 65:17; 66:22;** and **2 Peter 3:13?**

3. In view of the fact that sin is often defined as alienation or separation from God, what significance do you see in the phrase "coming down out of heaven from God" **(21:2)?**

4. Note that the new Jerusalem is described "as a bride beautifully dressed for her husband" **(21:2).** What does the New Jerusalem symbolize?

5. **Revelation 21:3–4** interprets the vision of the new creation. To what aspects of this new creation do the following passages point forward?
   a. **Exodus 25:8**

   b. **Leviticus 26:12**

   c. **Psalm 126:5**

   d. **Isaiah 25:8**

   e. **Isaiah 35:10**

   f. **Ezekiel 48:35**

g. **2 Corinthians 5:17**

h. **2 Corinthians 6:16**

6. How can we already in this life experience a foretaste of this bliss?

7. What is promised by God in **21:5?** What does God mean when He promises to the thirsty water without price **(21:6; Isaiah 55:1–3; John 4:13–14)?** Who is the water of life? What judgment does God pronounce on all those who are not thirsty for this water of life, who reject it?

The Holy City

Read **Revelation 21:9–22:5.**

Even as one of the seven angels with the seven bowls announced the punishment of the great prostitute Babylon **(17:1),** so one of the angels with the seven bowls introduced John to the celestial Jerusalem, the holy city of God. The concept of the church being the bride of Christ is frequently used in Scripture **(Isaiah 62:1–5; Ephesians 5:25, 32).** Several things are said about this celestial city of which we now have a foretaste, but which we one day will enjoy fully and eternally.

It is a city, a community of people—God's people—living together in perfect peace, cooperation, and harmony.

It comes down out of heaven from God **(21:10).** Our alienation and separation from God will be utterly removed, and we will live in direct, close companionship with Him, the source of all life and joy.

It needs no created luminary. The glory of God gives it light. And its lamp is Jesus Christ Himself, who is all truth and wisdom and who illumines us in all truth and wisdom. Through His Gospel we even now are enlightened in that which is real and true; in heaven we will have perfect understanding **(Revelation 21:23–25; Isaiah 60:1, 3, 5, 19–20; John 1:3–5; 8:12)**.

The city is surrounded by a wall with 12 gates **(21:12–13)**. The high wall denotes perfect safety and security. The 12 gates (three on each side) represent the 12 tribes of ancient Israel. God chose them to be His people to witness to the nations concerning His grace and mercy. Through these gates will pass all those people who have been led to saving faith in Christ. These gates are not to shut people out but are to provide them entrance.

The wall rests on 12 foundations on which are inscribed the names of the 12 apostles **(21:14)**. The church rests on the foundation of the prophets and apostles whose testimony we have in Scripture. The inclusion of both the 12 tribes of Israel and the 12 apostles indicate the continuity and unity of the Old and New Testament people of God—a unity that centers in Christ. (See **Ephesians 2:19–20**.)

This city is a perfect cube—12,000 stadia in width, length, and height **(21:15–17)**. (This is one possible explanation of the dimensions: 3 [the Trinity] × 4 [the universe] × 10 × 10 × 10 [an indication of ultimate completeness and perfection].) The dimensions suggest the complete, perfect communion we will have with God, only a shadow of which we now experience.

The city is built with most precious stones and pure gold **(21:18–21)**, which suggest the infinite preciousness of this heavenly city. The avenues of pure gold probably also symbolize our absolute purity in heaven, as well as the ready access we have to the throne and to the river and tree of life.

In the new Jerusalem there will no need for temples and churches; the people of God will fellowship with God directly **(21:22)**.

Believers from every nation will live in this new city. All activity will center in it. All that which is evil will be entirely excluded from it. In this perfect society the gates of the city need not be closed to keep out intruders bent on doing mischief **(21:25–27)**.

This city will be paradise restored **(22:1–5)**. As this universe was created to be paradise, it may be that life in the heavenly Jerusalem will be much like it is here—but entirely without sin and its consequences. Life will be both perfect and eternal.

Jesus Is Coming!

Read **Revelation 22:6–21.**

1. Why must we take the contents of **Revelation** seriously **(22:6)**?

2. Why are we ever to be watchful for the Last Day **(22:7, 12, 20–21)**?

3. What blessed assurance do we have **(22:14, 20–21)**?

4. What serious warning must we heed **(22:15, 18–19)**?

5. What power do we have to enable us to remain faithful in spite of all discouragements, opposition, and temptation **(22:17, 21)**?

Behold, I am coming soon! My reward is with Me, and I will give to everyone according to what he has done. I am the Alpha and the Omega, the First and the Last, the Beginning and the End. Revelation 22:12–13

REVELATION
Interpreting the Prophecy

Leaders Notes

Leaders Notes

Preparing to Teach Revelation

Group Bible Study

Group Bible study means mutual learning from one another under the guidance of a leader or facilitator. The Bible is an inexhaustible resource. No one person can discover all it has to offer. In a class, many eyes see many things, and can apply them to many life situations. Leaders should resist the temptation to "give the answers" and thereby take on the role of an "authority." This approach stifles participation by individual members and can actually hamper learning. As a general rule, the leader is not to give interpretation, but to *develop interpreters*. Of course, there are times when leaders should and must share insights and information gained by their own deeper research.

The ideal class is one in which the leader guides class members through the lesson, engages them in meaningful sharing and discussion at all points, and leads them to a summary of the lesson at the conclusion. As a general rule, try to avoid telling learners things that they can discover by themselves.

Have a chalkboard and chalk or newsprint and marker available to note significant points of the lesson. Recast your observations about the lesson, or the observations of participants, into questions, problems, or issues. This stimulates thought and reflection. Keep discussion to the point. List on the chalkboard or newsprint the answers given. Then determine the most vital points made in the discussion. Ask additional questions to fill obvious gaps.

The aim of every Bible study is to help people grow spiritually, not merely in biblical and theological knowledge, but in Christian thinking and living. This means growth in Christian attitudes, insights, and skills for Christian living. The focus of this course must be the church and world of our day. The guiding question will be, "What does the Lord teach us for life today through the book of **Revelation**?"

Teaching the New Testament

Teaching a New Testament letter that was originally written for and read to first-century Christians can become merely ancient history if not applied to life in our times. Leaders need to understand the time and culture in which the letter was written. They need to understand the historical situation of the early church and the social and cultural setting in which that church existed. Such background information can clarify the original purpose and meaning of the letters and shed light on their meaning for Christians today. For this reason, it would be good to consult a number of commentaries and Bible reference works in preparation for class.

Teaching the Bible can easily degenerate into mere moralizing, in which do-goodism or rules become substitutes for the Gospel, and sanctification is confused with justification. Actually, justified sinners are moved, not by Law, but by God's grace to a totally new life. Their faith is always at work for Christ in every context of life. Meaningful personal Christianity consists in a loving trust in God that is evidenced in love for others. Having experienced God's free grace and forgiveness, Christians daily work in their world to reflect the will of God for people in every area of human endeavor.

Christian leaders are Gospel-oriented, not Law-oriented: they distinguish between the two. Both Law and Gospel are necessary. The Gospel will mean nothing unless we first have been crushed by the Law and see our sinfulness. There is no genuine Christianity if faith is not followed by lives pleasing to God. In fact, genuine faith is inseparable from life. The Gospel alone gives us the new heart that causes us to love God and our neighbor.

Pace Your Teaching

Do not try to cover every question in each lesson. This would lead to undue haste and frustration. Be selective. Know your class members and pace your teaching accordingly. Take time to explore the biblical text, but do not focus on every minute detail. Rather, get the sweep and continuity of meaning. Stop occasionally to help participants gain understanding of a word or concept. Encourage members to study the text at home and report their findings at the next session. The time gained can be used to apply the lesson to life.

Should your group have more than a one-hour class period, you can ease the pace and proceed with more leisure. But do not allow any lesson to "drag" and become tiresome. Keep things moving. Keep the class alive. Keep the lesson meaningful.

Good Preparation

Good preparation by the leader usually affects the pleasure and satisfaction the class will experience. The student or teacher cannot get the background—historical, cultural, and theological—for **Revelation** by reading only the biblical text. Paragraphs, sentences, phrases, individual words and expressions can be understood fully only in light of the times and circumstances in which the apostle wrote. Thus it is important that both student and class leader consult introductory articles in reference works and commentaries. Also read the text in another translation.

Parishes should provide leaders with some essential books by purchasing them for the church library or for the individual teacher's library. The following resources are especially recommended:
- a good, recently revised Bible dictionary or encyclopedia;
- a thorough Bible commentary;
- one or more recent translations and paraphrases of **Revelation**: NIV, GWN, NRSV, Phillips, *The Living Bible*.

Personal Preparation

Good teaching directs learners to discover for themselves. For the leader, this means directing learners, not giving answers. As you prepare, mark those sections which suggest an activity most suitable for your class. Choose verses that should be looked up in Scripture. Decide which discussion questions you will ask, and to which you will devote the most time Write these in the margins of your Leaders Guide. Highlight the Study Guide questions you'll emphasize. What practical actions could you propose for the week following the lesson? Which questions in the Study Guide do you feel are most appropriate for your class? Mark these in your book.

Plan brief opening and closing devotions. Either use the suggestions provided in the Leaders Guide, or make up your own devotions. As much as possible—especially after the first sessions, when participants may still feel uncomfortable—involve class members in these devotions.

How will you best use your teaching period? Do you have 45 minutes? An hour? Or 1 1/2 hours? If time is short, what should you cut? Learn to become a wise steward of class time.

Perhaps most important of all, be sure to begin your preparations for each session—and the class sessions themselves—with personal prayer. Ask for God's wisdom, direction, and insight so that your mind is freed to focus on the biblical material and what it says to your life. When the text becomes clear to you, when John's revelation has meaning for your *life*, you will find it exciting—exhilarating—to help your class members discover how this letter speaks to them.

Suggestions for Using the Study Guide

The Study Guide material is designed to aid Bible study: that is, to aid a consideration of the written Word of God, with discussion and personal application growing out of the text at hand. Don't hesitate to alter the suggestions or to substitute other ideas that will better meet your own needs and the needs of the participants. Adapt your teaching plan to your own class and your class period.

Lesson 1
Introducing Revelation and Its Author

Central Truth

By the inspiration of the Holy Spirit, God has provided His people with the book of **Revelation,** the comforting message of hope in the face of persecution. Although evil and Satan run rampant in this present age, God is still in control; the exalted Christ is present among His people and rules all things for the ultimate welfare of His followers.

Objectives

That by the power of the Spirit working through the Word, the students will

1. identify the human author of **Revelation** and the original recipients of this letter;

2. describe the circumstances of the original recipients that created a need for this letter;

3. identify at least two purposes the author sought to achieve through this letter;

4. describe circumstances today similar to those of first-century Christians that make this letter relevant for Christians in our day;

5. describe apocalyptic literature;

6. demonstrate their understanding of the symbolic language and numbers used in **Revelation;**

7. understand the cyclical structure of **Revelation.**

Notes to the Leader

This lesson consists of background information necessary for a proper understanding of **Revelation.** As a class read through the information carefully, taking time to discuss it as students wish. Consult some of the reference materials listed in the study guide for more information on topics of interest to students.

Who Wrote Revelation?

1. The Bible passages clearly identify the writer as John.

2. Some Bible scholars have suggested that the author of **Revelation** might be John Mark (the writer of the second gospel; see **Acts 12:12, 25; 13:5, 13; 15:37**) or a later John the Elder who is not mentioned in the Bible. But the overwhelming view is that this John is John the apostle who

also wrote the gospel and the three epistles that bear his name. This course follows the traditional view that John the apostle authored **Revelation.** Have participants read through the information given about the apostle John, adding anything else they recall from Scripture.

a. John was the brother of the apostle James. These brothers were the sons of Zebedee and had been engaged in the fishing business with their father. When Jesus called them, they left without delay to follow Him **(Mark 1:19–20).**

b. John, together with James and Peter, was an eyewitness to the transfiguration of Jesus **(Luke 9:28–29).**

c. There was a special bond between John and Jesus. John reclined next to Jesus at the Last Supper. John is referred to as "the disciple whom Jesus loved" **(John 13:23).**

d. Because John was known to the high priest, he was able to follow Jesus into the high priest's courtyard on the night before His death **(John 18:15).**

e. Jesus gave the care of His mother over to John upon His death, and John took Mary into his home **(John 19:26–27).**

f. John outran Peter to the tomb on the first Easter morning **(John 20:1–10).**

g. John was the first to recognize the risen Lord when he appeared to the disciples on the Sea of Tiberias **(John 21:1–7).**

h. After Pentecost, John was with Peter at the healing of the man at the temple **(Acts 3:1–10).**

Primary sources for John's later life are Irenaeus (ca. 130–200), especially in his polemical writings against the Gnostics, and Eusebius (ca. 260–340). Tradition indicates that after years of leadership in the Jerusalem church, John moved to Ephesus. This likely occurred sometime shortly after the beginning of the Jewish revolt against Rome in A.D. 66 which culminated in the destruction of Jerusalem (A.D. 70). In the 90s, the Roman emperor Domitian (A.D. 81–96) launched a vigorous persecution of Christians. John was exiled to the island of Patmos, where he wrote the book of **Revelation.** Upon the death of Domitian, emperor Nerva permitted John to return to Ephesus. Trajan succeeded Nerva in A.D. 98, during whose reign John died. Church father Irenaeus stated that in his old age John was too weak to speak with his former vigor. As John was carried to meetings of the church, he supposedly encouraged the Christians by repeating, "Little children, love one another."

3. Have students look up the listed passages to note the supernatural, divine source of John's visions which he wrote "in the Spirit" **(1:10).**

For Whom Was Revelation Written?

Invite participants to skim the paragraphs that begin this part of the lesson. If time is short, commend the text to their private study and read the last paragraph ("However, the majority of scholars . . ."). Ask students to look up the Bible references to the seven churches in **Rev. 2:1, 8, 12, 18; 3:1, 7, 14.** Have students locate on the map in the study guide the seven cities addressed by John and the island of Patmos from where he wrote the letter. Refer them to an appropriate map in the back of their Bibles if they need help. Point out the inset on the map that shows the province of Asia in relation to the rest of the Mediterranean region.

The Purpose of the Letter

Throughout history the followers of God have been called on to suffer and die for their faith. This was true already in the Old Testament (see **Matt. 5:12; 23:37**). Jesus warned His disciples of all eras about the cost of discipleship **(Matt. 10:17–39).** He Himself was killed by those whom He came to deliver from the tyranny of sin, death, and hell. The first Jerusalem Christians met violent opposition (see the book of **Acts**). Briefly survey the persecutions of Christians throughout human history. Recall the crass persecution of Christians in the 20th century in the former East Germany and the former Soviet Union. Note also the subtle ways that Christians are persecuted in Canada or the United States when they seek to reflect their faith in everyday life. Emphasize that a major purpose of **Revelation** is to encourage Christians to remain steadfast in their faith in spite of opposition, ridicule, and persecution. A second purpose is to stimulate Christians to be energetic in fulfilling the missionary opportunities of the church in view of the horrendous future that awaits all who reject the Gospel of Christ and in view of the wonderful, blissful future that lies ahead for all the people of God.

Type of Literature

Point out that many people are intimidated by **Revelation** or misunderstand it because they lack understanding of its distinctive literary qualities and its use of symbolic language and numbers. Note that in the rest of this lesson, students will be introduced to those explanations necessary to properly understand, interpret, and apply this book to their Christian faith and life.

After reading through the information in this section, discuss with your class both the similarities and the differences between **Revelation** and apocalyptic literature in general.

The Symbolic Language of Revelation

Throughout your study of **Revelation,** you will encounter a variety of unfamiliar symbols. In the appropriate places these symbols will be explained. But it is desirable for your students at the outset to be prepared to meet with this symbolic language.

Use of such language is rather common today. For example, we speak of the Chicago Bears or the St. Louis Cardinals. Immediately we think of a football or baseball team—not animals. So in John's day people undoubtedly recognized immediately the figures of speech he used. You may think of other examples of symbolic language intelligible to your class that we use today.

For Discussion

1. Examples of "Babylon" in our contemporary world are those governments that persecute Christians. Discuss student responses.

2. Though subtle, forms of persecution of the people of God exist even in countries that permit the free exercise of religion. Examples include the scheduling of sporting events on Sunday mornings, exposure to a media that mocks Christ and His followers, and peer pressure to break God's commandments.

3. God promises His power so that nothing will be able to separate us from His love in Christ Jesus our Lord **(Rom. 8:35–39).**

The Use of Numbers

A major pitfall in the study of **Revelation** lies in the interpretation of the numbers found within it. The study guide describes some understandings of the symbolism of numbers in **Revelation.** At appropriate places throughout the course additional information will be given to help you interpret in a responsible fashion numbers as used by John.

Preparing to Lead

Understanding the cyclical structure of the book is crucial to its proper interpretation. Please give special attention to this aspect of the book. Each cycle covers the period from Christ's earthly ministry until He comes again on the Last Day.

An important key to understanding the imagery and message of **Revelation** is to understand the Old Testament references John uses. Throughout this study, give special attention to Old Testament passages listed in the study guide and to others listed in your Bible's cross reference system or in other materials you consult.

Reference Materials

If possible, obtain several commentaries for reference as you work through the study. Students are likely to have questions that are not covered in the study guide. It will enhance your study to have several different sources to consult about such questions.

For Next Time

Encourage students to become familiar with the outline of Revelation and to read **Rev. 1:1–3:22.** You can be of most assistance to students in their study, if you work through the next lesson prior to your next session.

Lesson 2

Preparing for the Truth

Bible Basis
Rev. 1:1–3:22

Central Truth

Even as the divine Jesus reigned also while on the cross, so His people live and reign in and with Him even in the midst of suffering and death.

Objectives

That by the power of the Spirit working through the Word, the students will

1. identify three ways John prepared his readers for his message;
2. explain the symbolic language used in **Revelation 1;**
3. describe the structure of the letters to the churches;
4. discuss the specific circumstances and needs of each of the churches;
5. identify the individual message given to each of the seven churches; and
6. apply the messages to the seven churches to the church of today.

Prolog and Doxology

1. After reading **Rev. 1:1–3,** discuss the questions in the study guide.

a. The ultimate source is God who, in His Son Jesus Christ, gave this revelation by His angel. The angel was commissioned by Jesus to guide

John in his visions of heaven, of earth, of the wilderness, and of the new heaven and new earth (see also **Rev. 1:10; 4:1; 10:4, 8; 19:9; 22:8–9**).

b. The purpose was to show John and, through him, other believers "what must soon take place." Those who read and heed this prophecy will be blessed, especially when the days of crisis draw near.

c. Christians are encouraged to remain steadfast in spite of persecution **(2:10)** and to anticipate eagerly the Second Coming of Jesus **(22:20).**

d. The angel revealed the visions to John who, in turn, bore witness to the Word of God and the testimony of Jesus Christ that he had received.

e. For John's immediate hearers the crisis likely was the persecutions they were enduring or soon would be enduring. To greater and lesser degrees, every generation since has also faced persecution in its time. Ultimately, the crisis is the great affliction that will precede the Second Coming of Jesus.

2. In **Rev. 1:4–8,** we have a beautiful description of the source of all revelation, God. God likely chose seven churches to indicate that His message is for all churches of every time and place.

3. The "who is, and who was, and who is to come" of **Rev. 1:4** is the great I AM of **Ex. 3:14,** the eternal Father, Lord of past, present, and future, the Creator and foundation of all things. All times, past and future, are embraced in His eternal present, which in part will shortly be revealed to John.

4. Jesus, the "faithful witness, the firstborn from the dead," is the martyr par excellence. The Greek word for witness, *martus,* came to be used by the persecuted church to refer to those who witnessed to the truth of God unto death. Hence the meaning of the English word *martyr.* Jesus was a "faithful witness" to the truth of God and as a result experienced the tyranny of evil in His own suffering and death. But He rose again, becoming "the firstborn from the dead." And He is and always has been "the ruler of the kings of the earth," using them to carry out His purposes.

5. By virtue of His substitutionary life, suffering, death, and resurrection Christ has freed us all from our sins and has made us "a kingdom and priests to serve His God and Father." This echoes **Ex. 19:6** where, after freeing Israel from the tyranny of Egypt, God tells them that they will be for Him "a kingdom of priests and a holy nation" (see also **1 Peter 2:5, 9**).

Because of Jesus' atoning work, all believers are part of His kingdom and share in His rule over all nations. Christians are priests not only because they through Christ can approach God directly but also because through their witness to and proclamation of the Gospel, the Holy Spirit mediates to all people the salvation gained by Jesus.

6. The rule of Christ over all will become evident to everyone when

Jesus visibly returns to earth on the clouds to bring this age to a close.

7. Those who have rejected Jesus and His salvation will mourn because finally they will understand their true condition before God as sinful people and will see that in rejecting Jesus they have rejected the gracious salvation offered by God and now face only God's judgment.

8. *Alpha* is the first letter of the Greek alphabet; *Omega* is the last. Saying that God is the Alpha and the Omega is a way of expressing His control over all of human history. He is before all things and gave them their beginning, and He will bring this world to an end.

9. Discuss the comfort that this section gives Christians, especially those who experience persecution and are tempted to doubt that God really is in control. The world does not now acknowledge the reign of Jesus over all things. But a major reason for the giving of **Revelation** was to enable its readers to see beyond outward circumstances and thus be encouraged by reality as seen from the perspective of God and His angels. At the end, all people will see the eternal realities. But in the meantime, Jesus comes to the world through the Gospel proclaimed by Christians to reveal what is and ever will be.

John's Call to His Prophetic Mission

1. The voice told John to write what he had seen, what is now and what is to happen in the future.

2. John fell as though dead at the figure's feet. Great respect and awe was shown by this action.

3. Jesus told John, "Do not be afraid. I am the First and the Last. I am the Living One; I was dead, and behold I am alive for ever and ever! And I hold the keys of death and Hades" **(1:17–18).**

4. The appearance of the figure and the sound of His voice all point to the fact that this is Jesus, but the words spoken to John in **1:17–18** confirm that it is He.

This picture of Jesus is rich in Old Testament imagery. In a vision, Ezekiel heard the voice of God, and it too sounded "like the roar of rushing waters" **(Ezek. 43:2).** Jesus here resembles an angel whom Daniel saw in a vision **(Dan. 10:5–6).** In another vision, Daniel also saw "one like a son of man" who received "authority, glory and sovereign power" from the Ancient of Days **(Dan. 7:13–14).** Interested participants may wish to read Daniel's entire vision in **Dan. 7:9–14.**

The Ancient of Days **(Dan. 7:9–14)** is God the Father, and in Daniel's vision He is the one who has white hair. In **Revelation,** Jesus has white hair. This might be an indication of the fact that Jesus shares the Father's eternal glory and that the Father has given Jesus the authority to rule His kingdom for Him.

Some of the descriptions of Jesus are repeated in the letters of **chapters 2–3** and will be discussed in connection with them.

5. The seven stars symbolize the angels of the seven churches. It is not entirely clear who these angels are. Some scholars think that they represent heavenly beings, perhaps the church's guardian angels. But the fact that the letters to the churches are addressed to these angels might indicate that they represent the pastors of the congregations. The seven lampstands are the seven churches themselves. Note that they are only lampstands; Jesus Himself is their light. Be sure that students read the concluding paragraph of this section in the study guide.

Jesus, the Son of Man, is to be found among the lampstands. Although He went to heaven at His ascension to be crowned in glory, Jesus is still present with His angels among His congregations on earth to bless them and finally lead them home into glory.

The Letters

Note the six common elements that appear in the seven letters. Their purpose was to prepare these believers for any trials that might befall them because of their faith, to reassure them of their close relationship with Christ and the hosts of heaven, to sustain and strengthen them in their ordeals, and to encourage them with the assurance that this present age will one day dissolve and that an eternal age of blessedness awaits all of the people of God.

Ask participants to read each letter with these elements in mind.

Ephesus

1. Jesus "holds the seven stars in His right hand and walks among the seven golden lampstands." Christ rules the angels of these churches (the seven stars) and is present in the midst of these churches (seven golden lampstands).

2. The Ephesian Christians worked hard, persevered in the midst of suffering, and were uncompromising over against evil. In their concern for truth, they tested those who claimed to be apostles (who claimed to have been sent by the Lord) but were not. And the Ephesians hated the deeds of the Nicolaitans. We know little about the Nicolaitans, but they seem to have been antinomians. Professing to be Christians, they yet indulged in various immoral practices.

3. Jesus reprimanded this church for forsaking its first love. In their zeal for truth, the Ephesians seemed to have become loveless in their attitudes toward and relationships with one another and Christ.

4. Jesus exhorted the Ephesians to recall what they were like before they forsook their first love, to repent, and to do what they had done before. If the Ephesians failed to repent, Jesus would remove their lampstand. A church may teach the Word faithfully, but in its "dead orthodoxy" and lack of love it may nevertheless self-destruct.

5. To those who by the power of the Spirit overcome (persevere in faith to the end), Jesus promises the gift of eternal life ("to eat from the tree of life").

6. Give students opportunity to apply this message to the church of today. Note that Jesus calls us to love but also to hate evil deeds.

Smyrna

1. Jesus is the First and the Last, the ever-living one who is all in all. He is the one who died and rose again for our eternal salvation and life.

2. These Christians endured poverty (the Greek indicates extreme poverty), ridicule, and afflictions because of their faith. Yet they remained steadfast in their faith and profession.

3. Eventually these believers might have become so discouraged because of their persecutions that they would have given way to Satan and forsaken the Savior.

4. Possibly the encouragement to remain faithful even unto death.

5. To those who by the power of the Spirit remain faithful unto death, God would give the crown of eternal life. Such people would not be harmed by the second death—eternity in hell.

6. Provide students opportunity to apply this to their lives.

Pergamum

1. Here Jesus "has the sharp, double-edged sword"—probably the Word that is a word of salvation to those who live in Christ, but a word of judgment and condemnation to those who deny or reject Him.

2. In the past these Christians had demonstrated their faithfulness to Jesus even when one of their number was martyred.

3. People who held to the teaching of Balaam were tolerated. Balaam was the prophet who was hired by Balak, the king of Moab, to curse the Israelites. The Lord instead had Balaam bless the Israelites. So Balaam suggested to Balak that he entice the Israelites to engage in sexual immorality and Baal worship. Thus they would bring God's judgment on themselves. Evidently there were some in the congregation at Pergamum who advocated indulging in sexual immorality and idolatry. There were also some who followed the Nicolaitans (see the letter to the Ephesians).

4. Unless the church repented of its tolerance of these false teachers

and their practices, Jesus would wield the sword of the Law—judgment and condemnation against the false teachers. Part of the church's mission is to call people to repentance and to withhold fellowship from them if they do not repent. The church does no favors to people by tolerating their unrepentant sin.

5. To those who overcome, Jesus will give "hidden manna"—Himself, the bread of life **(John 6:33, 35)** and a "white stone." We don't know for sure exactly what this white stone symbolizes, but perhaps holiness, beauty, forgiveness, and glory that will endure forever. In biblical times, a person's name represented his or her character. When God gives us a new name, He is giving us a new character.

6. Many applications can be given in an age when many people advocate and are involved in immorality and idolatry. Some even seek to be identified with God and the church and yet pursue self-fulfillment regardless of the divine will.

Thyatira

1. Jesus' "eyes are like blazing fire," symbolizing His righteous indignation because of what He in His omniscience knows to be amiss. His "feet are like burnished bronze"; He would stamp out all enemies of the truth.

2. Jesus noted their deeds, love, faith, service, and perseverance—and the fact that they had improved since they first came to faith.

3. Jezebel was the wife of King Ahab of Israel. She led many of God's people to sin by advocating the worship of Baal **(1 Kings 16:31; 18:19).** Like Jezebel, a prominent woman in this congregation was misleading people by advocating sexual immorality and eating meat offered to idols. She also promoted a kind of deep, secret "knowledge," perhaps an early form of Gnosticism.

4. This section **(2:20–24)** is an obvious call for those who followed the teachings of this woman to repent. Those who did not following her teachings were encouraged to hold on to what they had.

5. Jesus promises those who remain faithful that they will rule with Him in the age to come. The reference to the morning star is unclear, but we can be sure that it is a precious gift that our Lord promises to those whose faith endures.

6. Encourage students to discuss applications to today.

Sardis

1. Jesus sends the sevenfold Spirit of God, upon whom our Christian faith and life depend, to guide and empower His church. He also sends the angels, or ministers, of His church (the "stars"; see **1:20**).

2. In spite of the deadness of this church, a few people still walked with Christ.

3. This church was dead. The people went through the motions of religion, but Jesus meant little to them.

4. "Remember, therefore, what you have received and heard; obey it, and repent" **(v. 3).** If they did not, Christ would unexpectantly come to bring judgment on them.

5. Christ acknowledged the few who remained spiritually alive and promised that they would walk with Him, dressed in white, symbolic of His righteousness. To all who overcome, Christ promises this white dress and that their names will never be removed from the book of life, that is, they will inherit eternal life. And Jesus will acknowledge them before His Father and the hosts of heaven.

6. Students will likely be able to cite examples of spiritual deadness today.

Philadelphia

1. "Holy and true" echoes the divine title *Holy One* (see **Is. 40:25; Hab. 3:3; Mark 1:24**). Jesus "holds the key of David"—He is the fulfillment of all the Old Testament messianic promises. He is the one who has the keys to the kingdom; it is only through Him that a person enters the family of God.

2. In spite of their weakness, these Christians kept Jesus' Word and remained faithful to Him in the face of the opposition of unbelieving Jews.

3. The "open door" in **3:8** may refer to the door of the kingdom or to the door of opportunity to witness for Jesus. If the latter is the case, the danger faced by the congregation may have been that they would not go through that door, that is, they may not have been as alive to their evangelistic opportunities as they could have been.

4. Jesus reminded the people that, in spite of their faithfulness, they too were susceptible to falling away. He warned them against a sense of false security.

5. Jesus promised to keep them safe in the hour of trial and promised those who endured that they would be pillars in the temple of heaven in which they would dwell securely forever. They would belong to God (bear His name), be citizens of His kingdom (bear the name of the new Jerusalem), and share in the glory of Christ's new, exalted name.

6. Encourage students to discuss applications to today.

Laodicea

1. Here Jesus is called "the Amen, the faithful and true witness." He is

the truth and witnesses to God's truth (**John 3:11; 14:6**). He, with the Father, is the supreme ruler of all creation.

2. Really none at all. This is the only congregation of the seven in which Jesus seems to find nothing to praise.

3. The people were not only tepid in their Christianity; they were content to be so. Because of their material prosperity, they found their security and contentment in their possessions and wealth. They even boasted of their affluence.

4. Jesus called upon this church to turn to Him to find the gold to make them spiritually rich, white clothes to cover their spiritual nakedness, and eye salve to heal their spiritual blindness. Jesus suggested that He might have to discipline and rebuke them to move them to repent, but He would do it in love.

5. Christ offered to enter the hearts and lives of these people to bless them and to give them the right to sit with Him on the throne of glory.

6. Applications to life today should be easy to make.

For Next Time
Encourage students to read **Rev. 4:1–5:14.**

Lesson 3

Setting the Stage

Bible Basis
Rev. 4:1–5:14

Central Truth
Because of His redemptive life and work, Jesus now is the Mediator through whom we can approach the very throne of God.

Objectives
That by the power of the Spirit working through the Word, the students will

1. affirm the significance that the setting of **Revelation 4–5** has for a proper understanding of the book of **Revelation;**

2. describe the scene before the throne of God and the significance of

the various persons, objects, events, and symbols found in this scene;

3. identify similarities between the vision of John in **Revelation 4** and visions of Isaiah and Ezekiel;

4. compare the symbolic language used in **Revelation 4** with that used in other portions of Scripture;

5. describe the scroll and its significance;

6. describe the significance of the Lamb; and

7. affirm a desire to worship the Lamb in a thoughtful, meaningful manner.

Background

The inaugural vision before the throne of God in **Revelation 4–5** sets the tone for the entire book. Several thoughts are to be accented.

1. God on His throne rules all things. He controls everything for the welfare of the church so that it may accomplish the purposes for which God established it. He also blesses the Gospel wherever it is proclaimed. This is a source of comfort for us in times of trial and an encouragement to be faithful in sharing the Word.

2. Christ, seated at the right hand of the Father, dominates the book of **Revelation.**

3. In **chapter 5** we see the ascension of Jesus as viewed from heaven and His coronation to rule all things with the Father.

4. The foundation of all of **Revelation** is the sacrificial, saving life, suffering, death, and resurrection of Jesus Christ.

5. The heart of all of **Revelation** is the exalted reign of Christ. The prophecies of **Revelation** per se begin with **chapter 6.**

Before the Throne of God

Before the session, read **Revelation 4** and thoroughly digest the material given in this section of the study guide so that you will be able to lead the presentation and discussion fluently. Because of the nature of the material, most of this section is expository.

1–3. Read and discuss these questions in the study guide.

4. Discuss the similarities between John's vision and the visions of Isaiah and Ezekiel.

a. **Rev. 4:3/Ezek. 1:28**—In both cases a rainbow encircles God and His throne.

b. **Rev. 4:5/Ezek. 1:13**—In both cases lightning is present.

c. **Rev. 4:6/Ezek. 1:5**—In both cases four living creatures are present.

d. **Rev. 4:7/Ezek. 1:10**—In **Ezekiel** each creature has four faces: that of a man, a lion, an ox, and an eagle. In **Revelation** one creature is like a lion. One is like an ox. One has the face of a man. And the fourth flies like an eagle.

e.**Rev. 4:8/Ezek. 1:18; 10:12**—In both cases the living creatures are equipped with many eyes. In **Revelation** the creatures are covered with eyes. In **Ezekiel** each creature is associated with a wheel, the rim of which is full of eyes.

f. **Rev. 4:8/Is. 6:2**—In both cases the creatures have six wings. Those in Ezekiel's vision have four. In Isaiah the creatures are seraphim (seraphs), while those in Ezekiel are cherubim.

An Unending Hymn of Praise

Read and discuss this section.

1. The triple *holy* indicates the infinite holiness of God. You might suggest to students that they read through the hymn "Holy, Holy, Holy," noting the ways the words of the hymn echo the thoughts of this chapter of **Revelation.**

2. The elders praise God for creating all things by His will.

3. The God who gave us life sent His Son to offer us new life through Him. Our redemption was something only God could accomplish.

The Bible in Revelation

If time will allow, lead the students in a comparison of at least three of the sets of passages. One purpose is to lead students to an understanding of the unity and interrelatedness of all parts of the Bible—the Old Testament as well as the New. What John saw by revelation is the fulfillment of the promises in the Old Testament as well as in the New. If time is short, commend this section to the participant's personal study this week.

Who Is Worthy to Open the Scroll?

Read the material in this section. Encourage students to look up the Old Testament references.

"Worthy Is the Lamb"

1. The Lamb looked like He had been slain. As a sacrificial lamb, Jesus willingly laid down His life to pay for our transgressions.

2. Jesus has complete might and is in full control of the affairs of people.

3. The seven eyes represent the seven spirits (the Holy Spirit) sent out into the earth. Through the Holy Spirit, Jesus sees all things. One might see in this a reference to the Holy Spirit's role as being sent into the world to bring people to saving faith and to sustain believers in that faith.

4. Jesus was slain and with His blood He purchased people for God from

every tribe, language, people, and nation. He made all these people whom He purchased to be a kingdom and priests to serve God. And He enabled these people not only to serve God, but to reign with Him forever in the new earth.

5. The angels praise the Lamb by saying that He is worthy to receive seven things: power, wealth, wisdom, strength, honor, glory, and praise.

6. This material about the angels is interesting. Because angels are confirmed in their eternal bliss, we tend to think of them as beings superior to human beings. But in the order of God's creation, human beings are at the apex. The angels' function is to serve human beings as well as God. They are deeply interested in human beings and the salvation that Jesus gained for them. **1 Peter 1:10–12; Luke 15:10;** and **Heb. 1:14** describe aspects of this concern and the service of the angels for the welfare of human beings. So it is not strange that also in heaven they praise Jesus for the salvation and life He gained for humankind **(5:11–12).**

7. Human sin affects all creation (e.g., contemporary environmental problems). The redemption accomplished by Jesus Christ will bring restoration and renewal not only to the human family, but also to the entire created universe. See **Col. 1:20** and **Rom. 8:18–22.**

8. The praise of all creatures is directed to God the Father (who sits on the throne) and to Jesus, the Lamb. That Jesus receives the same praise as the Father emphasizes His divine nature.

For Reflection

These questions are designed to help participants internalize and apply the truths of the lesson to their personal lives.

For Next Time

Encourage students to read **Rev. 6:1–7:17.**

Lesson 4

The First Cycle of Tribulations: The Seven Seals

Bible Basis
Rev. 6:1–7:17

Central Truth
Although we may have to endure persecution and testing, we can be certain that God in Christ will keep us secure in the faith until we reach the heavenly goal.

Objectives
That by the power of the Spirit working through the Word, the students will

1. describe the cyclical character of the revelation given to John;
2. identify the meaning of each of the four horsemen;
3. give one answer as to why the righteous often suffer while the wicked prosper;
4. explain the significance of upheavals in nature and society in view of the Last Day;
5. state what the meaning of the sealing of the 144,000 means for their personal lives; and
6. describe their blessedness and hope as they anticipate the Last Day.

Introduction
The material in this section is basic for understanding the revelation of this book.

The Four Horsemen
Review the historical background of **Revelation** as given in the study guide. Throughout the early centuries pagans often blamed Christians for the problems of the world. They believed that the ancient gods were offended by the inroads of Christianity into the traditional order of things and were punishing humankind for deserting them. It was in defense of Christianity against this kind of accusation that St. Augustine wrote *The City of God* (written between A.D. 413 and 426).

1. The red horse and its rider symbolize war and bloodshed. No particular war is meant, but every war and rumor of war from the time of Jesus until the end.

2. The black horse and its rider depict famine and economic imbalance.

3. The pale horse pictures disease and death.

Point out that all of the things pictured will affect the world until its end.

4. Accept students' responses from history and the world today of situations created by each of the four horsemen.

5. Point out that the things are the result of sin in the world. God desires to give people salvation and to bless them with His good gifts regardless of their external circumstances.

The Fifth Seal

1. The first thing to note is the souls whom John sees under the altar of the heavenly tabernacle. They are believers who have died but are awaiting the final judgment. This supports the view that after death believers do not "cease to exist" nor "enter a state of sleep" until the judgment but are in a state of bliss between the time of death and resurrection. They do not fear the final judgment but long for it. While on earth, these saints were persecuted for their adherence to the word of God, yet they remained steadfast to the testimony of Jesus. This is most likely a reference to all believers who have died, those who experienced martyrdom as well as those who were persecuted and tempted to renounce their faith in more subtle ways and yet were faithful.

2. These souls are crying to be vindicated not out of spirit of vengeance, but because they know firsthand the pain caused by evil, and they long to see the triumph of God and His truth and justice. They long for evil to be punished and done away with forever. Their address to God acknowledges His power, holiness, and genuineness. They know that His truth will triumph; they just long for it to be soon.

3. In response to this plea each saint is given the personal robe of righteousness gained by Jesus Christ—the assurance that they are truly members of the great family of God. It is because they are clothed with Jesus' righteousness that they have no fear of the final judgment. Jesus bore their judgment for them.

They are reminded that the end will not come until their number is complete; that is, through the death of the martyrs God wins His victory over the powers of evil, and only complete, total victory will bring about the consummation of God's purpose.

The Great Earthquake

1. Have students look up the passages listed and note the descriptions of the end of the world. Allusions to these passages in this section of **Revelation** are obvious. Note the following points:

a. God will destroy all that proud and arrogant people have lifted up in idolatry **(Is. 2:12–22)**.

b. There will be no escaping the punishment of the Lord **(Is. 24:1–23)**.

c. In His wrath God will destroy the creation **(Is. 34:2–4)**.

You may want to extend the discussion to the false idealism of those who believe that people of themselves can create a perfect society in this age. Such efforts can be temporarily helpful, but ultimately they are futile. This world and all therein is passing away.

2. Note that Jesus lists wars **(Luke 21:9–10)** and earthquakes, famines, and pestilences **(21:11)** as preludes to the end. Jesus is describing the same things John saw in his vision of the horsemen. Then Jesus talks about persecution **(21:12)**. The souls that John saw under the altar had been persecuted. Be sure to note that all of these things will take place at various times until the end of the world. In **Luke 21:25–26,** Jesus describes a scene very much like John saw when the sixth seal was opened. This will happen at the very end of this era.

3. When the great upheavals in nature happen, Jesus will appear on a cloud with power and great glory and will send His angels to gather all of the elect.

4. The people of God are to be careful not to be weighed down by the temptations or cares of this world. They are to watch and pray so that they may be found faithful in the day of the coming of the Lord and thus may escape the terrible judgment faced by unbelievers. They will stand before Jesus and receive the acquittal He purchased for them with His blood.

The Sealing of the 144,000

Here we have the Christian church pictured as the New Israel—the chosen Israel of the New Testament era. Already in His ministry Jesus spoke of His disciples sitting "on twelve thrones, judging the twelve tribes of Israel" **(Matt. 19:28; Luke 22:30)**. Paul wrote that the believer in Christ is the true Israelite, or Jew **(Rom. 2:29)**. He referred to the church as "the Israel of God" **(Gal. 6:16)**. James addressed his letter to "the twelve tribes scattered among the nations" **(James 1:1),** and Peter used terminology from **Is. 43:20** and **Ex. 19:6** in referring to believers as "a chosen people, a royal priesthood, a holy nation" **(1 Peter 2:9).**

Encourage participants to look up the references in this section and to apply the passages to their lives. If time is short, read only two or three in class and commend the remaining passages to the participants for their own personal study this week.

The Song of Victory

Rev. 7:9–17 is one of the most familiar—and beautiful—sections of **Revelation.**

1. God's promise to Abraham was that his seed would be a great multitude that no one could number. The vision of heaven shows all of the spiritual seed of Abraham—"a great multitude that no one could count."

2. The palms point to the homage given Jesus already in Jerusalem on Palm Sunday. He is the promised Messiah in whom our sins have been cleansed (symbolized by the white robes) and through whose cleansing blood we now can appear before God.

3. Both **Psalm 98** and **Rev. 7:10, 12** are songs of praise to the Lord for the salvation He gives to all humankind.

4. We will serve God day and night in perfect happiness and bliss. We will never hunger, thirst, or experience pain or discomfort. God will wipe every tear from our eyes.

You might point out to students that **Rev. 7:14** is more correctly translated as follows: "These are they who are coming out of the great tribulation." This depicts the saints of God coming out of the tribulation of the world when they die. It does not support the teaching that Christians will be raptured out of the great tribulation that precedes the end of the world.

For Next Time

Encourage students to read **Rev. 8:1–9:21.**

Lesson 5

The Second Cycle of Tribulations: The Seven Trumpets

Bible Basis

Rev. 8:1–9:21

Central Truth

Although God permits Satan to seek the destruction of His created physical universe and of humankind, He still rules the universe and the course of human history in His infinite power and grace for the good of His people, His church.

Objectives

That by the power of the Spirit working through the Word, the students will

1. describe the importance of prayer in the reign of Jesus until the Last Day;

2. note the effects of sin on the physical world as indicated by the first four trumpet blasts;

3. describe the growing warfare on humankind by Satan and his followers;

4. describe the limitations that God places on Satan's assaults on humanity and the world; and

5. describe the rule of God's grace in a universe in which Satan and evil seem to be supreme.

Introduction

Because the cyclical structure of Revelation is so important for the proper understanding and interpretation of this book, use this introduction to review the nature and significance of the cycles.

Preparation for the Second Cycle

1. As Jesus rules during this period until the Last Day, He responds in His grace and wisdom to the prayers of His people on earth. As we live in a world filled with the woes of God's judgment, we have been sealed so that we might be safe, and we can commune with our Lord through prayer in the midst of the trials and tribulations that befall this world.

2. In **Joel** the trumpet announces the approach of the day of the Lord (the Last Day), a terrible day for unrepentant sinners. But until that day arrives people can still repent and return to the Lord who is gracious and merciful.

Nature Polluted

1. In **Rom. 8:19–22** Paul indicates that the entire physical universe suffers from the consequences of human sin. However, all of nature will be renewed when Jesus comes again to usher in the new heaven and the new earth.

2. Discuss student responses.

3. Catastrophic events in nature are signs of the end of this age. People can turn to the Lord for salvation. Those who call on His name will be saved.

4. That only a fraction is destroyed with each plague indicates that this punishment is not yet complete and final. The purpose of these visitations

is to warn people of the wrath and judgment of God and to bring them to repentance and saving faith. In His grace and mercy God is patient.

5. The people of God have nothing to fear from these catastrophic events because God is their refuge and the one who gives them strength. He controls such events, and nothing can take them away from Him.

6. The first set of passages uses darkness as a symbol of divine judgment. In **Col. 1:13** Paul uses darkness to symbolize the rule of sin and Satan to which people are enslaved apart from Christ.

7. Note the similarities between the plagues of Egypt and those preceding the Last Day.

a. Both include the plague of hail **(Ex. 9:13–35/Rev. 8:7)**.

b. Both include the turning of water into blood **(Ex. 7:14–24/Rev. 8:8–9)**.

c. Both include darkness **(Ex. 10:21–29/Rev. 8:12)**.

8. The Egyptian plagues preceded the exodus of God's people from the tyranny of Egypt to the Promised Land of Canaan. The plagues of **Revelation** precede the new exodus of God's people from the tyranny of this sinful world to the Promised Land of the age to come.

The Assault from the Abyss (The First Woe)

Discuss the material in this section.

The Reserves Are Brought In (The Second Woe)

1. By God's grace the church continues to teach the Word and administer the sacraments unhindered in many parts of the world. The church continues to grow even in those places where those who follow Christ are most severely persecuted.

2. We are part of the church. It is our privilege and obligation to reach out to others with the saving Gospel as God opens doors for us and empowers us. Ask students for examples of how God has used them to share the Good News with someone else.

For Next Time

Encourage students to read **Rev. 10:1–11:19.**

Lesson 6
"What's a Nice Person Like You Doing in This Kind of World?"

Bible Basis
Rev. 10:1–11:19

Central Truth
As God calls His people to share the Gospel of Jesus Christ in the face of opposition and hostility, He provides them with His presence and strength so that they may fulfill their mission with confident joy and hope.

Objectives
That by the power of the Spirit working through the Word, the students will

1. describe at least two purposes for which God has left them in this world filled with so much evil;

2. identify the Mighty One who has called them into mission;

3. point out why they can fulfill their mission in confidence;

4. understand why they can anticipate opposition and hostility as they seek to fulfill their God-given mission; and

5. explain why they can look toward the future, especially the end of their lives and of this world, with eager anticipation and joy.

Introduction
In the vision of the seven trumpets, John sees that which is to occur in church and society between the Lord's earthly ministry and the Last Day. Throughout the entire New Testament era God's people can expect to endure along with the world the results of sin in the form of calamities and death (although they are spared some of the suffering caused by the minions of Satan). In addition to general suffering, Christians can expect to suffer just because they are Christians. Here John prepares the people of God for the tribulations to come and gives them the assurance that the living Jesus will be with them to sustain and support them and finally receive them into eternal bliss with Him at the throne of heaven.

The One Who Calls Us
1. Twice before John had seen Jesus with His face like the sun, once earlier in **Revelation** and before that at the transfiguration.

2. The rainbow might point to God's covenant of gracious forbearance with the people of the earth.

3. The cloud and fiery pillars would remind John's readers of the pillar of cloud and pillar of fire by which God led the Israelites during the exodus and in the wilderness. So God continues to lead His people as they travel the road of the exodus from the evil of this age to the eternal holiness and glory of heaven.

4. In these passages, clouds symbolize the judgment of God on humankind as well as His majesty.

5. The appearance of this angel suggests that it was probably Jesus Himself. If not, it was an angel closely associated with Him for the fulfilling of His will. Note that in the Old Testament when God appeared in human form, He was often called "the angel of the Lord" (e.g., **Judg. 6:11–24**).

6. By placing His right foot on the sea and His left foot on the land, the angel indicates God's control over the whole world. As we will see in the following section, John is commissioned to carry God's message to many peoples. The posture of the angel here may be further indication that God's message is for the entire world. It must be heard by all, for this message of God will dominate all history. This is why God has placed us also in the world today. God has called us for this mission, even as he called John in **Revelation.**

The Purpose and Task for Which We Are Called

1. Ezekiel is commissioned to speak God's Word to the house of Israel. John's mission is to proclaim God's Word before many peoples, nations, languages, and kings.

2. This commission is essentially that which Jesus gave all His disciples. While we do not receive direct revelation as did Ezekiel and John, we, like they, are called to proclaim God's Word.

3. Eating the scroll symbolizes reading and internalizing its message. We must receive the Word and take it to heart before we can proclaim it.

4. That the scroll was sweet indicates joy in the promises of God. The Gospel of Jesus Christ itself is sweet and glorious. But the scroll also contains a word of judgment; its proclamation is often followed by bitter persecution and rejection.

5. We are to proclaim the Word of God to all people before the end of this age after which it will be too late for people to repent.

6. The Gospel of the kingdom will be preached to all nations before the end will come.

7. Give students time to verbalize how they today might fulfill their purpose in this world as Christians.

Confidence to Confess Boldly

Lead the students in a discussion of the material in this section. Take time to look up at least some of the Bible references listed. You may want to just skim the passages from **Ezekiel** and **Zechariah.**

The Church's Final Persecution and Triumph

1. The persecution will take place when the witnesses have finished their *testimony.* Recall Jesus' words and the similar vocabulary He used when He said that the Gospel must be preached in the entire world as a *testimony* to all nations and then the end would come **(Matt. 24:14).**

2. **Rev. 11:7** is probably relating the same thing as **Rev. 20:3,** in which case this beast is Satan, who comes up from the abyss where he has been held for the entire Gospel era until this time. Note that although Satan was bound, he was not powerless. He is ultimately the source of all the persecutions that have plagued the church throughout its history. Now he has been released for one final and direct onslaught.

3. The phrase "will attack them" in **Rev. 11:7** is more literally translated "will make war against them." This indicates that the church is a sizable enemy, but Satan overpowers and kills it. This does not necessarily mean that all believers living on earth are physically killed but that the church as a definable, witnessing community is destroyed. The church is dead and ineffectual.

4. Sodom symbolizes immorality and great sin. Egypt symbolizes rebellion against God and oppression of His people. Together with the reference to Jerusalem, these symbolize not one specific place but the world in opposition to God.

5. Refusing to bury someone is a sign of great contempt. Note that those gazing on the bodies of the witnesses come from the world over. Whereas past persecutions of the church were often localized, this persecution results in the worldwide death of the church.

6. Unbelievers break out in celebration over the death of the church because they were tormented by the church's message of repentance and forgiveness which called them to renounce their sins, their heresies, and their seeming control over their own lives. With the church dead they figure they can live as they please with no one to challenge them.

7. After a short period of time, the breath of God restores the church. This recalls Ezekiel's vision in which breath from God made dead bones live, symbolizing God's restoration of His people.

8. Those who witness the church's return to life are terrified because this vindicates the church's message and points to their condemnation.

The Day of Triumph

The seventh trumpet sounds. For unbelievers this is the sound of judgment and eternal torment and death. Justice is served.

But for the people of God who placed their trust for life and salvation not in themselves and their works, but in the saving life and work of Jesus Christ, the blast of the seventh trumpet announces the beginning of eternal glory. This is a fine positive note on which to end the session.

For Next Time

Encourage students to read **Rev. 12:1–14:20;** giving special attention to **chapter 12.**

Lesson 7

The Gathering Storm

Bible Basis

Rev. 12:1–17

Central Truth

Although Satan uses every possible means to destroy the church, God in Christ will enable His people to remain faithful even during times of hostility and opposition.

Objectives

That by the power of the Spirit working through the Word, the students will

1. identify the causes behind the outward struggle between the church and the world;

2. explain the symbolism and meaning of the vision of the dragon, woman, and child;

3. describe the significance of the war in heaven; and

4. express joy and confidence in the midst of opposition and hostility.

Introduction

Use the introductory material in the study guide to lay a foundation for the day's lesson.

Dragon, Woman, and Child

1. Sign—a great spectacle that points to the consummation of all earthly things. Jesus has told us that the Last Day will be preceded by the following: "great earthquakes, famines and pestilences in various places, and fearful events and great signs from heaven" **(Luke 21:11)**; "signs in the sun, moon and stars"; nations in "anguish and perplexity at the roaring and tossing of the sea" **(Luke 21:25)**; "wonders in the heaven above and signs on the earth below, blood and fire and billows of smoke" **(Acts 2:19)**.

2. The woman first represents the Old Testament people of God because it was from Israel that Christ came. After the child was born, the woman represents the church, the believers of the New Testament.

3. Although despised by the world, from God's point of view His people are radiant, glorious, and exalted. And He has allowed them to share His reign.

4. This male child will defeat Satan **(Gen. 3:15)**, will be God with us **(Is. 7:14)**, will be called "Wonderful Counselor, Mighty God, Everlasting Father, Prince of Peace" **(Is. 9:6)**. He will reign with power and might **(Ps. 2:9)**, and He is the Son of God, "born of a woman, born under law, to redeem those under law, that we might receive the full rights of sons" **(Gal. 4:4–5)**.

5. The dragon is Satan.

6. Not content with being creatures of God, certain angels wanted to be gods. They rebelled against Him to establish their own independence.

a. When these angels sinned, God condemned them to hell **(2 Peter 2:4)**.

b. These forces of evil continue to battle against the people of God **(Eph. 6:12)**.

c. God has kept the angels who rebelled against Him in darkness, "bound with everlasting chains for judgment on the great Day" **(Jude 6)**.

d. Our enemy, the devil, has always been and will always continue to be a murderer and a liar **(John 8:44)**.

e. Sinners are the servants of the devil, but Jesus came to destroy the work of the devil **(1 John 3:8)**.

7. The desert would have reminded John's readers of the desert in which the children of Israel lived for 40 years on their way to the Promised Land **(Ex. 16:1–10)**. There, God fed them with food from heaven and provided that their clothes did not wear out and their feet did not swell **(Deut. 8:2–5)**. Also, God provided for Elijah as he stayed by the brook when in the Kerith Ravine through ravens who brought Elijah bread and meat **(1 Kings 17:2–6)**. Another time when Elijah fled into the desert in order to escape Jezebel, God sent His angel to strengthen him **(1 Kings

19:2–9).

Perhaps John's reader were also reminded of the flight of Mary, Joseph, and the baby Jesus to Egypt **(Matt. 2:13–15)** or of Hosea's leading his wife into the desert to comfort and encourage her **(Hos. 2:14–15).**

8. Through the Word of God we have the saving knowledge of all that God in Christ has done for us. Plus we enjoy the fellowship of others who trust in Jesus and of the fellowship of the Father, and Christ as well. **(1 John 1:3).** We also enjoy grace and peace of our Lord, the love of God, and the fellowship of the Holy Spirit **(2 Cor. 13:11–14).**

War in Heaven

1. An example of Satan accusing the people of God can be found in the account of Job **(Job 1:6–12).** Satan stated that Job worshiped God only because of the material rewards he had received in return for his devotion. **Zech. 3:1** pictures Satan before God accusing Israel's High Priest at the time, namely Joshua, of having fallen short of God's standards. Joshua was able to stand because the Lord had taken away his sin **(3:4–5),** not because of his personal piety or perfection.

2. **Rev. 12:10–12** is a beautiful description of the victory over Satan and his accusations and the sure hope of eternal life with God won for us by Jesus through His life, death, and resurrection.

3. This hymn also includes a most solemn warning to those on earth against the determined efforts of Satan to destroy them.

4. In **Romans 8** Paul also confesses unequivocally that Satan cannot rightly bring any charge or condemnation against God's people because Christians are secure in the protecting grace of God. Nor can Satan separate them from God's love.

War on Earth

1. Even as God delivered His people from the tyranny of the Egyptians by carrying them on eagles' wings, so He gives the church eagles' wings to flee the tyranny of the devil. This symbolizes God's care for and protection of His people.

2. Satan will not only pursue the church as a whole but will make war on individual believers (her offspring).

3. God's people overcome Satan by the blood of Jesus, shed for their forgiveness, and the word of their testimony, that is, the Gospel which they share with others while here on earth. Note that they are even willing to give up their physical life in the struggle knowing that they will live forever with the Lord.

4. Summarize the session by giving students opportunity to identify

some of the problems they might expect because of their allegiance to Christ, but also the joy and confidence they have in God.

For Next Time

Encourage students to read **Rev. 13:1–14:20.**

Lesson 8

The War Intensifies

Bible Basis

Rev. 13:1–14:20

Central Truth

God, in His power and grace, allows those who trust in Him to live victorious over the powerful forces of evil around them that are bent on destroying their souls.

Objectives

That by the power of the Spirit working through the Word, the students will

1. describe how Satan uses tyrannical political powers to accomplish his deceptive and destructive goals;

2. describe how anti-Christian philosophies and religions seek the destruction of human souls;

3. describe the mission of the three angels;

4. describe the warning and the reassurance they receive from this lesson; and

5. praise God for His power and grace that enables them to live victoriously.

The Beast from the Sea

Revelation 13 shows us the instruments that the dragon (Satan) uses for his attack on the people of God.

1. Similarities between **Dan. 7:1–28** and **Rev. 13:1–10** are, among others, the following items:

a. Daniel saw four great beasts arise from the sea **(Dan. 7:3).** The beast of **Revelation** also emerged from the sea **(13:1)**.

b. One of the four beasts of **Daniel** was like a lion, one like a bear, and one like a leopard **(7:4–6)**. In **Revelation,** "the beast [John] saw resembled a leopard, but had feet like those of a bear and a mouth like that of a lion" **(13:2)**.

c. The fourth beast of **Daniel (7:7)** had ten horns. The beast of **Revelation** also had ten horns **(13:1)**.

Other similarities can be noted. Note the identification in **Daniel** of these beasts as political powers **(7:17)**.

2. The imagery of **Revelation 13** also appears elsewhere in the Bible as follows:

a. In both **Rev. 13:1** and **Is. 17:12** the *sea* represents the violent character of nations and political forces.

b. The *leopard* represents swiftness, cunning; it is large and fierce, swift to spring on its prey.

c. A *bear* is ready to rend and tear, eager with its great and terrible feet to crush the enemy.

d. The growling and roaring *lion*, eager to have its prey, is anxious to destroy.

3. The beast was given power to make war against God's people and conquer them.

4. Some examples of tyrannical powers in biblical times are Egypt, Assyria, Babylon, the Greece of Alexander the Great, Syria, and Rome. Located at the crossroads of the ancient world, Palestine was always vulnerable to the marching armies of the great powers. John was most likely thinking of Rome.

5. One notable example would be the former Soviet Union. It is interesting that in the Soviet Union and in China the church continued in spite of intense persecution. It went into hiding, to be sure, but it emerged perhaps stronger than ever.

6. Answers will vary.

7. One purpose is to bring people to repentance and faith. God's people may wander from Him. God permits affliction to happen in order to bring them back.

8. The passages cited are clear; the questions are designed for open discussion. Note that "Christians are obliged to obey civil authority. But when commands of the civil authority cannot be obeyed without sin, we "must obey God rather than men" **(Acts 5:29)**.

9. To worship this beast would mean to place one's trust for one's highest good in the political, economic, and social institutions of this world rather than in God.

10. As we have seen before in **Revelation,** the phrase "all inhabitants of the earth" refers to unbelievers. This verse makes that clear beyond a doubt by noting that those who worship the beast are those whose names are not written in the Lamb's book of life. By inference, those whose names are written there (believers) do not worship the beast.

11. The passages cited are clear; the questions are designed for open discussion.

The Beast out of the Earth

1. That the beast has two horns like a lamb might indicate that this beast appears to be like Christ. At the least the appearance of this beast is of a meek creature.

2. The voice of the beast, which is like that of a dragon, gives the beast away. In truth the beast is ferocious and destructive like the dragon—Satan.

3. Jesus warns us to watch out for false teachers. Although they are ferocious wolves (ready to devour their prey), they appear as meek and harmless as sheep. But they can be recognized for who they are by the products of their teaching.

4. This beast is antithetical to the Holy Spirit. The Holy Spirit leads people to confess and believe, "Jesus is Lord" **(1 Cor. 12:3).** Although false teachers do not always serve political authority (as the cult of emperor worship supported Rome in John's day), many times they do. In all cases they lead people away from trust in God to trust in human power, human philosophy, or human structures.

5. The second beast deceives with "great and miraculous signs" **(Rev. 13:13).** Jesus tells us in **Matt. 24:23–24** that false Christs and false prophets will deceive people with "great signs and miracles."

6. The beast will only be able to deceive the inhabitants of the earth, that is, the unbelievers. Note that in **Matt. 24:24,** Jesus indicates that these false prophets would deceive even the elect, but that is not possible.

7. The consequence of refusing to worship the image of the first beast is death. Not having the mark of the beast makes it impossible for believers to trade, meaning that they would not be able to function in that economic system, even to buy food. Christians should not be surprised if their loyalty to Christ leads them to economic ruin or even to death.

The Triumph of the Saints

1. We have encountered the number 144,000 before in **Revelation (7:4).** Here as there it stands for all the people of God from Adam and Eve down to those believers living at the Last Day. (The 144,000 equals the Old

Testament believers represented by the 12 tribes of Israel times the New Testament believers represented by the 12 apostles times 1,000, the number that indicates ultimate perfection and completeness.) Not one of God's chosen people, regularly nourished by the Spirit through the Word, will be lost to Satan.

2. Jesus' name and the Father's name are written on the foreheads of the saints; that is, they belong to God and the Lamb.

3. These saints are virgins, that is, by the power of the Spirit they persevered in their faithfulness to Christ.

The Mission of the Angels

1. **Luke 17:26–30** suggests that many people are lost because in this life they are so preoccupied with everyday activities that they ignore God and their eternal welfare.

2. Examples of indifference to warnings of judgment and the Gospel include materialism, disrespect for God's Word and the holy ministry, declines in church membership, preoccupation with self-satisfaction. Poor Bible study habits, "Sunday" Christianity, lack of zeal for mission work, and poor stewardship all indicate complacency on the part of the people of God. This spirit can be overcome only by the power of the Spirit of God, who works in human hearts through the Word and the sacraments.

3. Answers will include times students can reach out with the Word of God especially to those who in their absorption with the challenges and charms of this world are unconcerned and indifferent about their future and eternal well-being.

4. It is difficult to endure patiently, obey God's commandments, and remain faithful to Jesus because the temptations around us are so great. Opinion may vary as to whether it is more difficult today to persevere than in former ages. End this discussion on a note of assurance that God who is faithful gives His people the strength to persevere in faith.

The Final Harvest

1. In this age God permits the weeds (unbelievers) to grow with the grain (believers). However, at the end of this world in His divine and final judgment God will separate the weeds from the grain. Both **Rev. 14:14–20** and **Matt. 13:24–30** tell of this.

2. Both **Dan. 7:13–14** and **Rev. 14:14** speak of Jesus as the Son of Man, a term Jesus preferred using when referring to Himself. In both passages the Son of Man comes on the clouds of heaven to judge and to receive universal and lasting dominion. The crown points to Him as the Messiah who has conquered and thereby earned the right to act in judgment. The sharp

sickle is the instrument of harvest and depicts the Son of Man as coming to harvest the earth in judgment.

3. Give students an opportunity to respond to this question if they would like to do so.

For Next Time
Encourage students to read **Rev. 15:1–16:21.**

Lesson 9

The Third Cycle of Tribulations: The Seven Bowls

Bible Basis
Rev. 15:1–16:21

Central Truth
Through human history and events, as well as through phenomena in the world of nature, God preserves and protects those who belong to Him through Christ and He pronounces judgment on those who oppose Him and oppress His people.

Objectives
That by the power of the Spirit working through the Word, the students will

1. explain why Christians can rejoice in the midst of those tribulations that God permits to befall the world as the consequences of human sin;

2. describe the glorious state of the saints in heaven;

3. tell how God uses disorders in nature to punish the enemies of His people;

4. recognize how God also uses political unrest for judgment on those who oppose Him and oppress His people; and

5. identify the message of hope all Christians have while living in the midst of a decaying world.

Introduction
It is good to review once again the cyclical structure of **Revelation** as an introduction to the third cycle. Each cycle depicts events that occur

from the time of Christ to His Second Coming, events that point to the end. Each cycle ends with a view of Judgment Day. However, each cycle approaches this from a somewhat different perspective. This third and final cycle emphasizes the final judgments to be poured out on humankind.

The Church Triumphant

1. The previous sign was the woman symbolizing God's people. The whole history of the church has been one of conflict between the offspring of the woman (the Savior, **Gen. 3:15**) and Satan and his followers. The sign of **Revelation 15** reveals God's judgments on the oppressors of His people. These plagues belong to the drama of the continuing conflict between the church and the world led by Satan.

2. The sea of **Rev. 15:2** may allude to the Red Sea through which the exodus from Egypt occurred. Following the exodus, the people of Israel watched as the sea was used by God to defeat their enemies. In **Revelation** we see standing next to this fiery sea, those who have come out of this world and who will now witness the judgment of God against their enemies.

3. This description of all believers who endure faithfully in spite of persecution refers back to **chapter 13.** These are those who did not worship the beast and his image and who did not receive his mark.

4. The song of Moses in **Exodus 15** celebrated the deliverance of the Israelites at the Red Sea, while the song of Moses and the Lamb in **Revelation 15** celebrates the deliverance of humanity through the sacrificial life, suffering, death, and resurrection of Jesus Christ. Both songs praise God for His mighty deeds of salvation and His majesty.

5. After the exodus God instructed Moses to build the tabernacle as His dwelling place among the Israelites **(Ex. 25:8–9).** During the travels of the Israelites in the desert, God dwelt within the tabernacle with its ark of the covenant **(Ex. 40:34–35).** Within this ark were kept the two tablets of the Law that Moses received on Mt. Sinai **(Deut. 10:5).** These tablets were called the "two tablets of the Testimony" **(Ex. 32:15),** hence the name of the tabernacle used in **Rev. 15:5.** Here we see the heavenly tabernacle, after which the earthly tabernacle was patterned. The use of this figure points out that the seven bowls are *God's* judgment on the unbelieving world.

6. Frequently throughout the Old Testament, clouds and smoke indicated God's presence and His glory. This visible sign of God's presence among His people appeared in the tabernacle and then in the temple. The holiness and majesty of the divine presence were so overwhelming that sinful humans were often not able to be in the same room.

7. The gold indicates the bowls are to be used for God's purposes. The bowls are full to indicate the fierceness and unmitigated character of God's wrath. It is everlasting wrath for it proceeds from the eternal God. This judgment is final and one that will endure throughout eternity.

Plagues of Nature

Unless students wish to review the plagues of Egypt, it is not necessary to read the **Exodus** passage. As a class you might compare the seven trumpets with the seven bowls.

There are close parallels between these two visions, but whereas the first four plagues of the trumpet cycle affect only part of the world, the plagues of the first four bowls affect the entire world. This fits with the emphasis on "last plagues" in **Rev. 15:1.**

1. Physical health, salt water, fresh water, and the sun are affected by the first four plagues.

2. Both **Rev. 16:1–9** and **Matt. 24:29–31** emphasize that catastrophes in the physical universe will be a sign that this age is passing away and that the Lord will return to make all things new.

3. The first plague hits those who bear the mark of the beast and worship his image **(Rev. 13:15–17).**

4. The third plague—which turns fresh water to blood—is a fitting judgment on the enemies of God who spilled the blood of saints and prophets.

5. Although these plagues are judgments of God on His enemies, until the final judgment, God's judgments also serve the purpose of leading people to repentance. However, we are again cautioned about expecting many to repent.

6. This question is for application to personal life. Students might emphasize remaining faithful to escape the judgment of God and being diligent witnesses in order that others too might escape by trusting in the only means of escape—Jesus who bore God's judgment for us.

Plagues among the Nations

Read and discuss this section with your students.

The End of All Things

1. Discuss the similarites between the visions.

a. Great voices in heaven proclaim the realization of the kingdom of God **(11:15)**; a great voice from the heavenly throne declares that God's purpose has been accomplished **(16:17).**

b. In **Rev. 11:19** we read that the heavenly temple of God is opened, and there are flashes of lightning, rumblings, peals of thunder, an earthquake, and a great hailstorm; in **Rev. 16:18, 21** we read that there are flashes of lightning, rumblings, peals of thunder, the greatest of all earthquakes, and tremendous hail.

2. The cup of God's wrath is symbolic of God's judgment. Babylon the Great, symbolizing all the enemies of God's people, must drink that cup, that is, they must receive God's judgment. Jesus drank the cup of God's wrath for us. Students will likely be able to answer this last question without looking up the **Matthew** passage; however, they should read it in this context. It is quite possible that Jesus was referring to the cup of God's wrath in the Garden of Gethsemane.

3. In spite of all the evidences of God's judgment on sin, many unbelievers persist in their unbelief and evil ways.

4. In **Rev. 16:9,** repentance is mentioned, so it must still be possible even though not likely. It is possible because the final judgment has not yet come. In **16:21** repentance is not mentioned—likely because it is no longer possible. The final judgment has come.

5. The curses of unbelievers indicate that they blame God for the judgments that befall them; they do not acknowledge that their sin brought the judgments. The believers on the other hand praise God for being just and true and thereby acknowledge that those who receive judgment do indeed deserve it. The marvelous deeds for which the believers praise God include their redemption from sin through Jesus and the judgment that they too would have had to bear had not Christ bore it for them.

6. A discussion question for personal application.

For Next Time

Encourage students to read **Rev. 17:1–18:24.**

Lesson 10

The Fall of Babylon

Bible Basis
Rev. 17:1–18:24

Central Truth
Although Babylon, the great enemy of God's people, continues to lure

people away from God and to shed the blood of His saints, the day of her total and complete destruction will surely come.

Objectives

That by the power of the Spirit working through the Word, the students will

1. identify the allurements of the great prostitute of **Revelation 17–18;**
2. flee her influence;
3. realize that their faithfulness to Christ may entail losing their lives;
4. recognize the control of God over all earthly events; and
5. rejoice in the destruction that will befall the great enemies of God.

Introduction

This paragraph and the boxed material on Babylon provides background on the imagery of Babylon. You will probably want to have participants skim the longer Old Testament passages rather than read them in their entirety. Or commend the passages to the students for personal study outside class.

The Prostitute and the Beast

1. Babylon is called a prostitute because she not only commits adultery, she entices others into adultery.

2. Adultery is a common Old Testament metaphor for idolatry and apostasy. God is the husband and His people the wife who is unfaithful. She prostitutes herself by worshiping idols and trusting in foreign powers rather than in God for her security.

3. The rulers of the earth and the inhabitants of the earth (unbelievers).

4. The inhabitants of the earth are drunk, that is, they are totally caught up in this adultery and they can't think clearly. In **18:23** Babylon's influence is described as a magic spell.

5. The attire of the prostitute exudes not only royalty (symbolized by the colors) but enormous wealth. And as we see from **chapter 18,** she shares that wealth with all who commit adultery with her.

6. The cup is filled with the abominable and filthy things. The allurements of the world in reality offer nothing but filth.

7. The prostitute's title reveals that this is indeed Babylon the Great and that she is not only a prostitute but that she brings forth other prostitutes and the abominations of the earth.

8. Babylon the Great not only sheds the blood of the saints (those who witness to Jesus), she revels in doing it and gets drunk on their blood.

9. The woman has influence throughout the world and will lead all nations astray.

10. This beast, the beast from the sea in **chapter 13,** symbolizes the civil governments of this world in their anti-Christian aspect.

11. Both **Revelation 13** and **Revelation 17** note the astonishment of the unbelievers.

12. According to **Rev. 17:8** this astonishment is called forth by the fact that the beast "once was, now is not, and yet will come." This aspect of the beast is pictured in **chapter 13** as the fatal wound that had healed. As in **chapter 13,** this symbolizes that when one anti-Christian government has fallen, another will rise in its place.

13. This description of the beast, along with his blasphemous names **(17:3),** indicates that this beast has placed himself in the position of God. The power and seeming invincibility of the beast draws forth the astonishment and allegiance of unbelievers. The beast comes from the abyss, which indicates his satanic origin.

14. This king, the beast himself, is going to his destruction.

15. The one purpose of these kings and the beast is to make war on the Lamb.

16. The Lamb will be victorious because He is "Lord of lords and King of kings" **(17:14).** He will be accompanied by His called, chosen, and faithful followers.

17. God accomplishes His purpose by letting the beast destroy the prostitute.

Babylon Has Fallen!

1. Although God's people must live in the world influenced by the prostitute, they are not to be taken in by her allurements. They are to separate themselves from her and refuse to share in her sins that they might not experience her judgment.

2. Babylon, great though she is, will fall in a very short period of time ("one day" in **18:8;** "one hour" in **18:10**).

3. They have lost their source of wealth and luxury, and they are terrified that her fate will befall them also.

4. Babylon will be completely and totally destroyed.

5. The reaction of the prophets, apostles, and saints of God (all God's people) is to be one of rejoicing because God has judged the great prostitute for shedding their blood.

For Next Time

Encourage students to read **Rev. 19:1–21.**

Lesson 11
The Victory Is Won

Bible Basis
Rev. 19:1–21

Central Truth
In the visions of the marriage of the Lamb and the rider on the white horse, Christians in every age are assured of Christ's final victory over all evil—a victory He shares with all His faithful followers.

Objectives
That by the power of the Spirit working through the Word, the students will

1. express joy in the future that they have in Jesus Christ;

2. praise God for His victory over all evil forces that seek to destroy His people;

3. explain how Christ's relationship with His people can be described as a marriage;

4. describe and explain the significance of the vision of the rider on the white horse; and

5. express personal assurance derived from the visions reported in **Revelation 19.**

The Victory Song
God's people praise God for His salvation, glory, and power and for justly condemning the great prostitute and thus avenging the blood of His saints which she spilled.

Marriage Feast of the Lamb
1. Reflect with your students on the following passages that use the bridegroom and bride imagery to tell of the relationship of the Lord and His people:

a. **Is. 62:5**—Here God is compared to a bridegroom who rejoices over His bride, the new Israel.

b. **Jer. 2:31–32**—Israel's unfaithfulness is compared to a bride who forgets her wedding ornaments.

c. **2 Cor. 11:2**—Here Paul writes of Christ as the husband and the church as this pure virgin.

d. **Eph. 5:25–32**—The relationship between husband and wife is compared to that of Christ and His church.

e. **Rev. 21:9–10**—The Lamb is compared to the bridegroom whose wife is the church.

2. The fine linen represents the righteousness bestowed on the people of God through the sacrificial blood of the Lamb.

3. The phrase "*given* her to wear" (italics added) emphasizes that our righteousness and our salvation are free gifts bestowed on us by God for the sake of the sacrificial life, suffering, death, and resurrection of our Savior, Jesus Christ.

4. Angels are creatures of God who worship and serve God. They are not to be worshiped. Only God is worthy of worship.

The Victor Receives His Victory

1. The rider on the white horse is Christ, who is completely faithful and true. Therefore, we can fully and safely entrust to Him our whole being and future. The whiteness of the horse indicates the purity of our Lord, a purity He also bestows on all His followers. Also, Christ will judge in purity and righteousness all those who rejected His gracious offer of salvation and life.

2. Jesus comes to judge in righteousness and justice all those who in this lifetime rejected His grace, forgiveness, and life. A person can choose to be judged either in justice or by God's grace in Christ. Those who choose justice will surely be condemned eternally because of their sin. But if by the power and wisdom of the Holy Spirit, people are led to rely on the redemption purchased for them by Christ, then they are assured of eternal life.

3. Christ will judge righteously and with omniscience.

4. The blood may be that of Christ's enemies whom He has vanquished. It might also be a reference to the blood that Jesus shed on Calvary for our salvation.

5. Jesus is God's own Word revealed to humanity. To know Jesus is to know God.

6. The sword is the Word of God. The Law condemns us for our sin. If we persist in living under the Law, we will perish because no human being can fulfill it. The Gospel reveals to us our Savior, and through it the Holy Spirit implants saving faith within us, sustains us in that faith, empowers us for holy living, and leads us safely amid all the temptations and troubles of this life to our eternal home.

7. The quotation and the name indicate that Jesus has absolute authority that no one can resist. He is Lord of all.

8. **Rev. 19:18** indicates the totality of the human enemies of God who will be defeated. None will be excluded.

9. Encourage students to discuss the meaning of **Revelation 19** for their personal lives of faith.

For Next Time

Encourage students to read **Rev. 20:1–15.**

Lesson 12

The Millennium

Bible Basis

Rev. 20:1–15

Central Truth

Although numerous millennial theories concerning the last times have been concocted over the years, Scripture clearly teaches that God will permit unbelief and evil to flourish in this world along with the faithful witness of God's people until Christ returns to inaugurate the new age for His followers.

Objectives

That by the power of the Spirit working through the Word, the students will

1. describe the classical Christian understanding of **Revelation 20;**

2. explain why they can be confident of eventual victory in spite of the growing opposition and hostility of Christ's enemies;

3. identify the grace of God in Christ as being the foundation for their confidence of eternal salvation; and

4. describe the various millennial theories and explain in what ways they are contrary to Scripture.

The Millennium

1. All of these passages contain the promise that God's kingdom and the salvation He has provided will spread throughout the world.

2. The passages describe aspects of the conflict between Jesus and

Satan that occurred during Jesus' earthly ministry.

a. Jesus resisted the devil's temptations **(Matt. 4:1–11; Luke 4:1–13)**.

b. Jesus cast out demons, but He would not let the demons speak because they knew who He was. The teachers of the law accused Jesus of using the devil's power to cast out these evil forces, but Jesus pointed out that Satan's house would be divided and fall if he fought against himself. In His illustration of tying up the owner of the house before robbing that house, Jesus described what He was doing to Satan; Jesus was binding Satan so that He could rob him of his power **(Mark 1:34; 3:20–30)**.

c. Jesus healed a man possessed by a legion of demons and cast the demons into a herd of swine **(Mark 5:1–20)**.

d. One time the demon in a possessed man cried out identifying Jesus as the "Holy One of God." Jesus then cast the demon out of the man **(Mark 1:21–28)**.

e. Though the prince of the world seemed to have triumphed with the death of Jesus on the cross, the death of Jesus was really the devil's defeat **(John 12:30–33)**.

3. The second resurrection is the bodily resurrection that will occur on the Last Day when the souls of all who have died will be reunited with their bodies.

4. The second death is eternal condemnation in hell.

Satan's Doom

Read and discuss this section.

The Great Judgment

Read and discuss this section. The great comfort to be found in **Rev. 20:14** is that death, which causes people such great suffering, will be destroyed forever.

Millennial Theories

1. In spite of our sin and unworthiness, our substitute, Jesus Christ, perfectly fulfilled God's Law on our behalf and endured the divine punishment for our sin. Therefore, we face Jesus' Second Coming and Judgment Day with the assurance that we are the people of God and heirs of heaven.

2. God has placed us in this world to care for it, seek its peace, and, above all, live as children of light and witness to God's saving work in Jesus Christ.

3. Upon our physical death we are with the Lord.

4. Christ's Second Coming will occur at the end of this age. He then will

raise all who have died. Believers will live forever with the Lord.

5. Christ's Second Coming will be sudden and unexpected; therefore all predictions of the time of His coming are futile. In fact, He has discouraged us from speculating by urging us to be ready at all times.

6. Rather then envision a millennium of peace and prosperity prior to the Second Coming, Scripture clearly and unequivocally affirms that evil and unbelief will abound in this world to the very end. The optimistic passages appealed to by millennialists foretell the spiritual glory of the New Testament church and the spread of the Gospel throughout the world.

7. Only one passage, **1 Thess. 4:13–17,** speaks unequivocally of the rapture. In this passage Paul's point is that at the Second Coming those who are then living will not have an advantage over those "who have fallen asleep."

8. **Rom. 11:25–26** does not teach that all Jews eventually will be saved even as it does not affirm the universal salvation of Gentiles. In **Rom. 9:6–8,** Paul specifically states that all Israel is not made up of the physical descendants of Abraham, but of all those who with Abraham place their trust in the promises of God as centered in Jesus Christ.

For Next Time
Encourage students to read **Rev. 21:1–22:21.**

Lesson13
The New Jerusalem

Bible Basis
Rev. 21:1–22:21

Central Truth
By God's grace, all who acknowledge their inability to save themselves and, by the Spirit's power, place their only hope for salvation in Jesus Christ and His saving work will reign forever with Christ in the new age, which He will inaugurate at the Last Day.

Objectives
That by the power of the Spirit working through the Word, the students will

1. acknowledge that perfect peace, prosperity, and security will be established only in the world that is to come after the Last Day;

2. describe the similarities between the first paradise **(Genesis 1–2)** and the paradise that is to come **(Revelation 21–22)**;

3. describe the new heaven and the new earth as depicted in **Revelation 21**;

4. describe the new Jerusalem as portrayed in **Revelation 21–22**; and

5. express an understanding of how they are to prepare for the final consummation of this age.

Introduction

1. **Gen. 1:1/Rev. 21:1**—God created the heavens and the earth/God will establish a new heaven and a new earth.

2. **Gen. 1:14–19/Rev. 21:23–25; 22:5**—God created light/in the new heaven and earth there will be no need for created light because the glory of God gives it light and the Lamb is its lamp.

3. **Gen. 3:1/Rev. 21:8**—Satan is cunning and succeeds/Satan's work is destroyed.

4. **Gen. 3:8/Rev. 21:3**—Humankind is alienated from God and flees from Him/humankind is redeemed and lives in closest fellowship with God.

5. **Gen. 3:16–19/Rev. 22:3**—Humanity and the earth are cursed because of Adam and Eve's sin/there is no more curse.

6. **Gen. 3:22/Rev. 22:14**—Sinful people are forbidden to eat of the tree of life/those who have washed their robes in the blood of the Lamb now eat freely of the tree of life.

7. **Gen. 3:22–24/Rev. 22:2**—Paradise is lost/paradise is restored.

A New Heaven and a New Earth

1. This present universe is decaying and passing away. Note the different ways in which the cited passages describe this impermanence.

2. John sees the fulfillment of a promise made by God centuries before Christ through the prophet Isaiah and looked forward to by Peter.

3. "Coming down out of heaven from God" describes how God Himself takes the initiative to reestablish the close relationship that existed between Himself and humanity in the Garden of Eden. In the new heaven and earth this intimate relationship between God and His people will continue forever.

4. Just as the church is sometimes described as the new Israel, here the new Jerusalem symbolizes the church, the bride of the Lamb. John may also have in mind a literal city that God will build in the new earth, or this

may be a completely figurative description of the holy Christian church.

5. Throughout the history of God's people, God used events and places and images and experiences to point forward to the new creation that would culminate that history. The passages point forward to the following aspects of the new creation:

a. God dwelling among His people

b. God being their God and making them His people

c. No more tears

d. The end of death; no more tears or disgrace

e. Joy and gladness forever; no more sorrow or sighing

f. God's eternal presence with His people

g. Those in Christ being made new

h. God's people being His temple (His dwelling place) and God being their God and making them His people

6. Already in this life, as we reflect on the words and promises of God, the Holy Spirit gives us inner peace and contentment. Students can give examples of times they felt especially close to God.

7. God promises to make our whole universe entirely new. We can count on it because His words are trustworthy and true. In this new heaven and earth, only perfect righteousness and peace will exist. This new universe is given to us to enjoy forever without price—it is the free gift of God's grace in Jesus Christ, our Savior, who is the water of life. The sin that condemns people to hell is to reject Jesus, the water of life.

The Holy City

Lead students in a discussion of this section.

Jesus Is Coming!

1. What was revealed to John is reality. We reject it to our own eternal destruction.

2. Jesus will return soon and suddenly, when we may least expect Him. In a real sense, He comes for each of us at the time of our physical death. Many people die with no advance warning. We are always to be prepared for Him when He comes to take us.

3. We are assured Jesus will come soon to take us into eternal blessedness.

4. All those who reject Christ and serve evil and Satan will be cast into eternal separation from God and everything that is good.

5. The Spirit of God and God's grace in Christ enable us to persevere in our relationship with God until Christ comes again to take us to be with Him forever.